Library of
Davidson College

"THE HIGHER CHRISTIAN LIFE"

SOURCES FOR THE STUDY OF THE HOLINESS, PENTECOSTAL, AND KESWICK MOVEMENTS

A forty-eight-volume facsimile series reprinting extremely rare documents for the study of nineteenth-century religious and social history, the rise of feminism, and the history of the Pentecostal and Charismatic movements

Edited by
Donald W. Dayton
Northern Baptist Theological Seminary

Advisory Editors

D. William Faupel, *Asbury Theological Seminary*
Cecil M. Robeck, Jr., *Fuller Theological Seminary*
Gerald T. Sheppard, *Union Theological Seminary*

A GARLAND SERIES

Late Nineteenth Century Revivalist Teachings on the Holy Spirit

with a Preface by
Donald W. Dayton
Northern Baptist
Theological Seminary

Garland Publishing, Inc.
New York & London
1985

231.3
L351

For a complete list of the titles in this series
see the final pages of this volume.

Preface copyright © 1985 by Donald W. Dayton

Library of Congress Cataloging-in-Publication Data
Main entry under title:

*LATE NINETEENTH CENTURY REVIVALIST TEACHINGS
ON THE HOLY SPIRIT.*

("The Higher Christian life")
Reprint (1st work). Originally published: Chicago :
F.H. Revell, 1881.
Reprint (2nd work). Originally published: Chicago :
F.H. Revell, 1894.
Reprint (3rd work). Originally published: Chicago :
F.H. Revell, 1877.
Contents: Secret power, or, The secret of success in
Christian life and work / D.L. Moody — Received ye the
Holy Ghost? / J. Wilbur Chapman — The baptism with the
Holy Spirit / R.A. Torrey.
1. Holy Spriit—Addresses, essays, lectures.
2. Baptism in the Holy Spirit—Addresses, essays,
lectures.   3. Christian life—Addresses, essays,
lectures.   I. Moody, Dwight Lyman 1837–1899. Secret
power, or, The secret of success in Christian life
and work.   1985.   II. Chapman, J. Wilbur (John Wilbur),
1859–1918. Received ye the Holy Ghost? 1985.
III. Torrey, R. A. (Reuben Archer), 1856–1928.
Baptism with the Holy Spirit.   1985.   IV. Series.
BT122.L38   1985   231'.3   85-20738
ISBN 0-8240-6412-7 (alk. paper)

The volumes in this series are printed on
acid-free, 250-year-life paper.
Printed in the United States of America

CONTENTS

Preface
Donald W. Dayton

*Secret Power, or
the Secret of Success in
Christian Life and Work*
D. L. Moody

Received Ye the Holy Ghost?
Wilbur Chapman

The Baptism with the Holy Spirit
R. A. Torrey

PREFACE

Late-nineteenth-century revivalism and popular evangelicalism were suffused with holiness themes. This fact is sometimes obscured by the later tendency to suppress such themes, especially after the emergence of Pentecostalism generated greater controversy about them. But it is clear that the broader evangelical traditions in America, especially those aspects most rooted in nineteenth-century revivalism, cannot be fully understood without attention to the influence of the holiness movement. Nor is it possible to understand the ease with which Pentecostalism spread after the turn of the century without noticing the extent to which pre-Pentecostal and near-Pentecostal doctrines permeated the international evangelical and missionary culture at the turn of the century.

Evangelist Charles Grandison Finney is generally considered the father of modern revivalism who initiated the "new measures" that have characterized revivalism down to the present practice of Billy Graham. Other volumes in this series (see especially volume 17, *Lectures to Professing Christians*, and volume 15 by James Fairchild, *Oberlin: The Colony and the College*, as well as volume 28

PREFACE

by Asa Mahan, *Out of Darkness into Light*) document the rise of "Oberlin Perfectionism" and its variation on the holiness teachings. The interpretation of Finney's teachings in this area, especially with regard to whether he taught a doctrine of the "baptism of the Holy Spirit" as a second experience, is still a matter of controversy. Early on Finney clearly taught the possibility of a form of Christian perfection, and his thoughts took greater shape in the late 1830s at Oberlin with the revival of interest in "entire sanctification." In various passages in his writings, especially occasional pieces in *The Oberlin Evangelist*, Finney uses Pentecostal imagery and speaks of a "baptism of the Holy Spirit." But it is not clear that Finney was as explicit as Asa Mahan, the first president of Oberlin, in making a clear connection between entire sanctification and the "baptism of the Holy Spirit." Finney used a variety of expressions and images, including the "infilling" or the "sealing" of the Spirit to describe a second experience, though he was also less insistent on the definitiveness and singularity of this second experience. By the time Mahan had clearly developed his doctrine of *The Baptism of the Holy Ghost* (1870) Finney was more inclined to speak of an "enduement with power"— an expression reflected in the title of an address he delivered to the first National Congregational Council meeting in Oberlin in November of 1871. This was apparently the kernel of an essay that was appended to the English edition of Mahan's book from the same period.

The latter-nineteenth-century revivalists reflect both the fascination with this theme and the fluidity of its

PREFACE

precise interpretation. In the 1870s Dwight Lyman Moody (1837–1899) became the preeminent evangelist of the late nineteenth century. In 1871 Moody experienced a form of spiritual depression which was eventually resolved in a crisis experience, in part under the prompting of two Free Methodist ladies who encouraged him to seek the empowerment of the "baptism of the Holy Spirit." Moody spoke of this experience somewhat reluctantly because of the controversies surrounding the issue, but when he did he used a variety of terms, including the anointing, the filling, the baptism, the unction, and the empowerment of the Spirit. Moody's teachings and the difficulty of categorizing them are revealed in his little book *Secret Power* (1881). His position is akin to that of Finney in emphasizing the theme of empowerment more than the sanctification themes of the holiness movement as such. By distinguishing in chapter II between "power in" all Christians and the "power upon" that was a subsequent form of Christian experience Moody found a middle path through the controversies.

Presbyterian evangelist John Wilbur Chapman (1859–1918) was a graduate of Oberlin and for a while associated with D. L. Moody before pursuing his own independent evangelism career with song leader C. M. Alexander. Chapman's teachings are illustrated in his little volume, *Received Ye the Holy Ghost?* (1894), significantly dedicated to Moody and F. B. Meyer, a prominent teacher of the British Keswick movement. Like Moody, Chapman placed the emphasis on empowerment and shied away from a doctrine of the "baptism of the Holy

Preface

Spirit," preferring instead to speak of an "infilling of the Holy Spirit."

But Rueben Archer Torrey (1856–1928), closely associated with the work of Moody and first superintendent of Moody Bible Institute, showed none of the reticence of Moody and Chapman about the expression "baptism with the Holy Spirit," as is indicated by his volume with that title here reprinted. Torrey accepted explicitly most features of the holiness doctrine of the baptism of the Spirit (especially its definiteness and its subsequence and distinction from conversion) but continued the revivalist emphasis on "empowerment" for witness and service as its primary function (rather than sanctification). All that is lacking here from the Pentecostal doctrine of the "baptism in the Spirit" is the experience of speaking in tongues as the evidence of having received this baptism, though it is clear from the notes on pp. 33–36 that Torrey would have been leery of the Pentecostal themes and in fact became a vicious critic of Pentecostalism once it emerged a few years later.

Donald W. Dayton
Northern Baptist
Theological Seminary

Revell's Premium Library

A neatly-bound series of reprints of favorite religious works, suitable for distribution as gifts and premiums. 16mo, cloth, each 50 cents.

Light on Life's Duties. By Rev. F. B. Meyer.
The Secret of Guidance. By Rev. F. B. Meyer.
Nobody Loves Me. By Mrs. O. F. Walton.
Select Poems. By various authors.
The Man who Spoiled the Music, and other Temperance Stories. Selected from various authors.
The Fall of the Staincliffes. Prize story on the Evils of Gambling. By A. Colbeck.
Good Tidings. Gospel Sermons.
Recitation Poems. By Mrs. Kohaus.
All of Grace. By Charles H. Spurgeon.
According to Promise. By Charles H. Spurgeon.
And Peter. By Rev. J. Wilbur Chapman, D.D.
Resurrection. A Symposium.
The Good Shepherd. The Story of Jesus, for Children. Illustrated.
God's Way of Peace. By Rev. Horatius Bonar, D.D.
How Shall I Go to God. By Rev. Horatius Bonar, D.D.
Point and Purpose in Story and Saying.
First Battles and How to Fight Them. By Frederick A. Atkins.
The Way of Life. Gospel Sermons.
Sowing and Reaping. By D. L. Moody.
The Way to God and How to Find It. By D. L. Moody.
To the Work! To the Work! By D. L. Moody.
Twelve Select Sermons. By D. L. Moody.
Prevailing Prayer—What Hinders It? By D. L. Moody.
Bible Characters. By D. L. Moody.
Heaven and How to Get There. By D. L. Moody.
Secret Power. By D. L. Moody.
Sovereign Grace. By D. L. Moody.
He's Coming Tomorrow. By Harriet Beecher Stowe.

SECRET POWER

OR THE

SECRET OF SUCCESS IN CHRISTIAN LIFE AND WORK

BY D. L. MOODY

FLEMING H. REVELL COMPANY
NEW YORK : : CHICAGO : : TORONTO
Publishers of Evangelical Literature

Copyrighted 1881, by FLEMING H. REVELL.

PREFACE.

One man may have "zeal without knowledge," while another may have knowledge without zeal. If I could have only the one, I believe I should choose the first; but, with an open Bible, no one need be without knowledge of God's will and purpose; and the object of this book is to help others to know the source of true power, that both their zeal and their knowledge may be of increased service in the Master's work.

Paul says, "all Scripture is given by inspiration of God, and is profitable;" but I believe one portion, and that the subject of this book, has been too much overlooked, as though it were not practical, and the result is lack of power in testimony and work. If we would work, "not as one that beateth the air," but to some definite purpose, we must have this power from on high. Without this power, our work will be drudgery. With it, it becomes a joyful task, a refreshing service.

May God make this book a blessing to many. This is my prayer.

D. L. MOODY.

NORTHFIELD, MASS., May 1st, 1881.

CHAPTER I.

POWER—ITS SOURCE.

In vain do the inhabitants of London go to their conduits for supply unless the man who has the master-key turns the water on; and in vain do we think to quench our thirst at ordinances, unless God communicates the living water of His Spirit.—*Anon.*

It was the custom of the Roman emperors, at their triumphal entrance, to cast new coins among the multitudes; so doth Christ, in His triumphal ascension into heaven, throw the greatest gifts for the good of men that were ever given.—*T. Goodwin.*

To unconverted persons, a great part of the Bible resembles a letter written in cipher. The blessed Spirit's office is to act as God's decipherer, by letting His people into the secret of celestial experience, as the key and clew to those sweet mysteries of grace which were before as a garden shut up, or as a fountain sealed, or as a book written in an unknown character.—*Toplady.*

The greatest, strongest, mightiest plea for the Church of God in the world is the existence of the Spirit of God in its midst, and the works of the Spirit of God are the true evidences of Christianity. They say miracles are withdrawn, but the Holy Spirit is the standing miracle of the Church of God to-day. I will not say a word against societies for Christian evidences, nor against those weighty and learned brethren who have defended the outworks of the Christian Church. They have done good service, and I wish them every blessing, but as to my own soul, I never was settled in my faith in Christ by Paley's Evidences, nor by all the evidence ever brought from history or elsewhere; the Holy Spirit has taken the burden off my shoulders, and given me peace and liberty. This to me is evidence, and as to the externals which we can quote to others, it was enough for Peter and John that the people saw the lame man healed, and they needed not to speak for themselves.—*Spurgeon.*

POWER—ITS SOURCE.

"Without the soul, divinely quickened and inspired, the observances of the grandest ritualism are as worthless as the motions of a galvanized corpse."—*Anon.*

I QUOTE this sentence, as it leads me at once to the subject under consideration. What is this quickening and inspiration? What is this power needed? From whence its source? I reply: The Holy Spirit of God. I am a full believer in "The Apostles' Creed," and therefore "I believe in the Holy Ghost."

A writer has pointedly asked: "What are our souls without His grace?—as dead as the branch in which the sap does not circulate. What is the Church without Him?—as parched and barren as the fields without the dew and rain of heaven."

There has been much inquiry of late on the subject of the Holy Spirit. In this and other lands thousands of persons have been giving attention to the study of this grand theme. I hope it will lead us all to pray for a greater manifestation of His power upon the whole Church of God. How much we have dishonored Him in the past! How ignorant of His grace, and love and presence we have been? True, we have heard of Him and read of Him, but we have had little intelligent knowledge of His attributes, His offices and His relations to us. I fear He has not been to many professed Christians an actual existence, nor is He known to them as a personality of the Godhead.

The first work of the Spirit is to give life; spiritual life. He gives it and He sustains it. If there is no life, there can be no power; Solomon says: "A living dog is better than a dead lion." When the Spirit imparts this life, He does not leave us to droop and die, but constantly fans the flame. He is ever with us. Surely we ought not to be ignorant of His power and his work.

IDENTITY AND PERSONALITY.

In John v, 7, we read: "There are three that bear record in heaven, the Father, the Word, and the Holy Ghost, and these three are one." By the Father is meant the first Person, Christ, the Word is the second, and the Holy Spirit, perfectly fulfilling His own office and work in union with the Father and the Son, is the third. I find clearly presented in my Bible, that the One God who demands my love, service and worship, has there revealed Himself, and that each of those three names of Father, Son and Holy Ghost has personality attached to them. Therefore we find some things ascribed to God as Father, some to God as Saviour, and some to God as Comforter and Teacher. It has been remarked that the Father plans, the Son executes, and the Holy Spirit applies. But I also believe they plan and work together. The distinction of *persons* is often noted in Scripture. In Matt. iii, 16–17, we find JESUS submitting to baptism, the SPIRIT descending upon Him, while the FATHER's voice of approval is heard saying: "This is my Beloved Son in whom I am well pleased." Again in John xiv, 16, we read: "I (*i. e.* Jesus) will pray the Father, and He shall give you another Comforter." Also in Eph. i, 18: "Through Him (*i. e.* Christ Jesus) we both (Jews and Gentiles) have access by one Spirit unto the Father." Thus we are taught the distinction of persons in the Godhead, and their inseparable union. From these and other scriptures also we learn the identity and actual existence of the Holy Spirit.

If you ask do I *understand* what is thus revealed in Scripture, I say "no." But my faith bows down before the inspired Word and I unhesitatingly believe the great things of God when even reason is blinded and the intellect confused.

In addition to the teaching of God's Word, the Holy Spirit in His gracious work in the soul declares His own presence. Through His agency we are "born again," and through His indwelling we possess superhuman power. Science, falsely so called, when arrayed against the existence and presence of the Spirit of God with His people, only exposes its own folly to the contempt of those who have become "new creatures in Christ Jesus." The Holy Spirit who inspired prophets, and qualified apostles, continues to animate, guide and comfort all true believers. To the actual Christian, the personality of the Holy Spirit is more real than any theory science has to offer, for so-called science is but calculation based on human observation, and is constantly changing its inferences. But the existence of the Holy Spirit is to the child of God a matter of Scripture revelation and of actual experience.

Some skeptics assert that there is no other vital energy in the world but physical force, while contrary to their assertions, thousands and tens of thousands who can not possibly be deceived have been quickened into spiritual life by a power neither physical or mental. Men who were dead in sins—drunkards who lost their will, blasphemers who lost their purity, libertines sunk in beastliness, infidels who published their shame to the world, have in numberless instances become the subjects of the Spirit's power, and are now walking in the true nobility of Christian manhood, separated by an infinite distance from their former life. Let others reject, if they will, at their own peril, this imperishable truth. I believe, and am growing more into this belief, that divine, miraculous creative power resides in the Holy Ghost. Above and beyond all natural law, yet in harmony with it, creation, providence, the Divine government, and the upbuilding of the Church of God are presided over by the Spirit of God. His ministration is the ministration of life more glorious than the ministration of law, (2 Cor. iii, 6–10). And like the Eternal Son, the Eternal Spirit having life in Himself, is working out all things after the counsel of His own will, and for the everlasting glory of the Triune Godhead.

The Holy Spirit has all the qualities belonging to a person; the power to understand, to will, to do, to call, to feel, to love. This can not be said of a mere influence. He possesses attributes and qualities which can only be ascribed to a person, as acts and deeds are performed by Him which can not be performed by a machine, an influence, or a result.

AGENT AND INSTRUMENT.

The Holy Spirit is closely identified with the words of the Lord Jesus. "It is the Spirit that quickeneth; the flesh profiteth nothing, the words that I speak unto you, they are spirit and they are life." The Gospel proclamation can not be divorced from the Holy Spirit. Unless He attend the word in power, vain will be the attempt in preaching it. Human eloquence or persuasiveness of speech are the mere trappings of the dead, if the living Spirit be absent; the prophet may preach to the bones in the valley, but it must be the breath from Heaven which will cause the slain to live.

In the third chapter of the First Epistle of Peter, it reads, "For Christ also hath once suffered for sins, the just for the unjust, that He might bring us to God, being put to death in the flesh, but quickened by the Spirit."

Here we see that Christ was raised up from the grave by this same Spirit, and the power exercised to raise Christ's dead body must raise our dead souls and quicken them. No other power on earth can quicken a dead soul, but the same power that raised the body of Jesus Christ out of Joseph's sepulcher. And if we want that power to quicken our friends who are dead in sin, we must look to God, and not be looking to man to do it. If we look alone to ministers, if we look alone to Christ's disciples to do this work, we shall be disappointed; but if we look to the Spirit of God and expect it to come from Him and Him alone, then we shall honor the Spirit, and the Spirit will do His work.

SECRET OF EFFICIENCY.

I can not help but believe there are many Christians who want to be more efficient in the Lord's service, and the object of this book is to take up this subject of the Holy Spirit, that they may see from whom to expect this power.

In the teaching of Christ, we find the last words recorded in the Gospel of Matthew, the 28th chapter and 19th verse, "Go ye, therefore, and teach all nations, baptizing them in the name of the Father, and of the Son, and of the Holy Ghost." Here we find that the Holy Spirit and the Son are equal with the Father—are one with Him, "teaching them in the name of the Father, and of the Son, and of the Holy Ghost." Christ was now handing His commission over to His Apostles. He was going to leave them. His work on earth was finished, and He was now just about ready to take His seat at the right hand of God, and He spoke unto them and said: "All power is given unto Me in heaven and on earth." All power, so then He had authority. If Christ was mere man, as some people try to make out, it would have been blasphemy for Him to have said to the disciples, go and baptize all nations in the name of the Father, and in His own name, and in that of the Holy Ghost, making Himself equal with the Father.

There are three things: *All power* is given unto Me; go *teach all* nations. Teach them what? To *observe all* things. There are a great many people now that are willing to observe what they like about Christ, but the things that they don't like they just dismiss and turn away from. But His commission to His disciples was, "Go teach all nations to observe all things whatsoever I have commanded you." And what right has a messenger who has been sent of God to change the message? If I had sent a servant to deliver a message, and the servant thought the message didn't sound exactly right—a little harsh—and that servant went and changed the message, I should change servants very quickly; he could not serve me any longer. And when a minister or a messenger of Christ begins to change the message because he thinks it is not exactly what it ought to be, and thinks he is wiser than God, God just dismisses that man.

They haven't taught "all things." They have left out some of the things that Christ has commanded us to teach, because they didn't correspond with man's reason. Now we have to take the Word of God just as it is; and if we are going to take it, we have no authority to take out just what we like, what we think is appropriate, and let dark reason be our guide.

It is the work of the Spirit to impress the heart and seal the preached word. His office is to take of the things of Christ and reveal them unto us.

Some people have got an idea that this is the only dispensation of the Holy Ghost; that He didn't work until Christ was glorified. But Simeon felt the Holy Ghost when he went into the temple. In 2d Peter, i, 21, we read: "Holy men of old spake as they were moved by the Holy Ghost." We find the same Spirit in Genesis as is seen in Revelation. The same Spirit that guided the hand that wrote Exodus inspired also the epistles, and we find the same Spirit speaking from one end of the Bible to the other. So holy men in all ages have spoken as they were moved by the Holy Ghost.

HIS PERSONALITY.

I was a Christian a long time before I found out that the Holy Ghost was a person. Now this is something a great many don't seem to understand, but if you will just take up the Bible and see what Christ had to say about the Holy Spirit, you will find that He always spoke of Him as a person—never spoke of Him as an influence. Some people have an idea that the Holy Spirit is an attribute of God, just like mercy—just an influence coming from God. But we find in the fourteenth chapter of John, sixteenth verse, these words: "And I will pray the Father, and He shall give you another Comforter that He may abide with you forever." That *He* may abide with you forever. And, again, in the same chapter, seventeenth verse: "Even the Spirit of Truth, whom the world can not receive, because it seeth Him not, neither knoweth Him; but ye know Him; for He dwelleth with you and shall be in you." Again, in the twenty-sixth verse of the same chapter: "But the Comforter, which is the Holy Ghost, whom the Father will send in my name, He shall teach you all things, and bring all things to your remembrance whatsoever I have said unto you."

Observe the pronouns "He" and "Him." I want to call attention to this fact that whenever Christ spoke of the Holy Ghost He spoke of Him as a person, not a mere influence; and if we want to honor the Holy Ghost, let us bear in mind that He is one of the Trinity, a personality of the Godhead.

THE RESERVOIR OF LOVE.

We read that the fruit of the Spirit is love. God is love, Christ is love, and we should not be surprised to read about the love of the Spirit. What a blessed attribute is this. May I call it the dome of the temple of the graces. Better still, it is the crown of crowns worn by the Triune God. Human love is a natural emotion which flows forth towards the object of our affections. But Divine love is as high above human love as the heaven is above the earth. The natural man is of the earth, earthy, and however pure his love may be, it is weak and imperfect at best. But the love of God is perfect and entire, wanting nothing. It is as a mighty ocean in its greatness, dwelling with and flowing from the Eternal Spirit.

In Romans v, 5, we read: "And hope maketh not ashamed, because the love of God is shed abroad in our hearts by the Holy Ghost which is given to us." Now if we are co-workers with God, there is one thing we must possess, and that is love. A man may be a very successful lawyer and have no love for his clients, and yet get on very well. A man may be a very successful physician and have no love for his patients, and yet be a very good physician; a man may be a very successful merchant and have no love for his customers, and yet he may do a good business and succeed; but no man can be a co-worker with God without love. If our service is mere profession on our part, the quicker we renounce it the better. If a man takes up God's work as he would take up any profession, the sooner he gets out of it the better.

We can not work for God without love. It is the only tree that can produce fruit on this sin-cursed earth, that is acceptable to God. If I have no love for God nor for my fellow man, then I can not work acceptably. I am like sounding brass and a tinkling cymbal. We are told that "the love of God is shed abroad in our hearts by the Holy Ghost." Now, if we have had that love shed abroad in our hearts, we are ready for God's service;

if we have not, we are not ready. It is so easy to reach a man when you love him; all barriers are broken down and swept away.

Paul when writing to Titus, second chapter and first verse, tells him to be sound in faith, in charity, and in patience. Now in this age, ever since I can remember, the Church has been very jealous about men being unsound in the faith. If a man becomes unsound in the faith, they draw their ecclesiastical sword and cut at him; but he may be ever so unsound in love, and they don't say anything. He may be ever so defective in patience; he may be irritable and fretful all the time, but they never deal with him. Now the Bible teaches us, that we are not only to be sound in the faith, but in charity and in patience. I believe God can not use many of his servants, because they are full of irritability and impatience; they are fretting all the time, from morning until night. God can not use them; their mouths are sealed; they can not speak for Jesus Christ, and if they have not love, they can not work for God. I do not mean love for those that love me; it don't take grace to do that; the rudest Hottentot in the world can do that; the greatest heathen that ever lived can do that; the vilest man that ever walked the earth can do that. It don't take any grace at all. I did that before I ever became a Christian. Love begets love; hatred begets hatred. If I know a man loves me first, I know my love will be going out towards him. Suppose a man comes to me, saying, "Mr. Moody, a certain man told me to-day that he thought you were the meanest man living." Well, if I didn't have a good deal of the grace of God in my heart, then I know there would be hard feelings that would spring up in my heart against that man, and it would not be long before I would be talking against him. Hatred begets hatred. But suppose a man comes to me and says, "Mr. Moody, do you know that such a man that I met to-day says that he thinks a great deal of you?" and though I may never have heard of him, there would be love springing up in my heart. Love begets love; we all know that; but it takes the grace of God to love the man that lies about me, the man that slanders me, the man that is trying to tear down my character; it takes the grace of God to love that man. You may hate the sin he has committed; there is a difference between the sin and the sinner; you may hate the one with a perfect hatred, but you must love the sinner. I can not otherwise do him any good. Now you know the first impulse of a young convert is to love. Do you remember the day you was converted? Was not your heart full of sweet peace and love?

THE RIGHT OVERFLOW.

I remember the morning I came out of my room after I had first trusted Christ, and I thought the old sun shone a good deal brighter than it ever had before; I thought that the sun was just smiling upon me, and I walked out upon Boston Common, and I heard the birds in the trees, and I thought that they were all singing a song for me. Do you know I fell in love with the birds? I never cared for them before; it seemed to me that I was in love with all creation. I had not a bitter feeling against any man, and I was ready to take all men to my heart. If a man has not the love of God shed abroad in his heart, he has never been regenerated. If you hear a person get up in prayer-meeting, and he begins to speak and find fault with everybody, you may know that his is not a genuine conversion; that it is counterfeit; it has not the right ring, because the impulse of a converted soul is to love, and not to be getting up and complaining of every one else, and finding fault. But it is hard for us to live in the right atmosphere all the time. Some one comes along and treats us wrongly, perhaps we hate him; we have not attended to the means of grace and kept feeding on the word of God as we ought; a root of bitterness springs up in our hearts, and perhaps we are not aware of it, but it has come up in our hearts; then we are not qualified to work for God. The love of God is not shed abroad in our hearts as it ought to be by the Holy Ghost.

But the work of the Holy Ghost is to impart love. Paul could say, "The love of Christ constraineth me." He could not help going from town to town and preaching the Gospel. Jeremiah at one time said: "I will speak no more in the Lord's name; I have suffered enough; these people don't like God's word. They lived in a wicked day, as we do now. Infidels were creeping up all around him, who said the word of God was not true; Jeremiah had stood like a wall of fire, confronting them, and he boldly proclaimed that the word of God was true. At last they put him in prison, and he said: "I will keep still; it has cost me too much." But a little while after, you know, he could not keep still. His bones caught fire; he had to speak. And when we are so full of the love of God, we are compelled to work for God, then God blesses us. If our work is sought to be accomplished by the lash, without any true motive power, it will come to nought.

Now the question comes up, have we the love of God shed abroad in our hearts, and are we holding the truth in love? Some people hold the truth, but in such a cold stern way that it will do no good. Other people want to love everything, and so they give up much of the truth; but we are to hold the truth in love; we are to hold the truth even if we lose all, but we are to hold it in love, and if we do that, the Lord will bless us.

There are a good many people trying to get this love; they are trying to produce it of themselves. But therein all fail. The love implanted deep in our new nature will be spontaneous. I don't have to learn to love my children. I can not help loving them. I said to a young miss some time ago, in an inquiry meeting, who said that she could not love God; that it was very hard for her to love Him —I said to her, "Is it hard for you to love your mother? Do you have to learn to love your mother?" And she looked up through her tears, and said, "No; I can't help it; that is spontaneous." "Well," I said, "when the Holy Spirit kindles love in your heart, you can not help loving God; it will be spontaneous." When the Spirit of God comes into your heart and mine, it will be easy to serve God.

The fruit of the Spirit, as you find it in Galatians, begins with love. There are nine graces spoken of in the sixth chapter, and of the nine different graces Paul puts love at the head of the list; love is the first thing—the first in that precious cluster of fruit. Some one has put it in this way: that all the other eight can be put in the word love. Joy is love exulting; peace is love in repose; long suffering is love on trial; gentleness is love in society; goodness is love in action; faith is love on the battlefield; meekness is love at school; and temperance is love in training. So it is love all the way; love at the top; love at the bottom, and all the way along down these graces; and if we only just brought forth the fruit of the Spirit, what a world we would have; there would be no need of any policemen; a man could leave his overcoat around without some one stealing it; men would not have any desire to do evil. Says Paul, "Against such there is no law;" you don't need any law. A man who is full of the Spirit don't need to be put under law; don't need any policemen to watch him. We could dismiss all our policemen; the lawyers would have to give up practicing law, and the courts would not have any business.

THE TRIUMPHS OF HOPE.

In the fifteenth chapter of Romans, thirteenth verse, the Apostle says: "Now the God of hope fill you with all joy and peace in believing, that you may abound in hope through the power of the Holy Ghost." The next thing then is hope.

Did you ever notice this, that no man or woman is ever used by God to build up His kingdom who has lost hope? Now, I have been observing this throughout different parts of the country, and wherever I have found a worker in God's vineyard who has lost hope, I have found a man or woman not very useful. Now, just look at these workers. Let your mind go over the past for a moment. Can you think of a man or woman whom God has used to build His kingdom who has lost hope? I don't know of any; I never heard of such an one. It is very important to have hope in the Church; and it is the work of the Holy Ghost to impart hope. Let Him come into some of the churches where there have not been any conversions for a few years, and let Him convert a score of people, and see how hopeful the Church becomes at once. He imparts hope; a man filled with the Spirit of God will be very hopeful. He will be looking out into the future, and he knows that it is all bright, because the God of all grace is able to do great things. So it is very important that we have hope.

If a man has lost hope, he is out of communion with God; he has not the Spirit of God resting upon him for service; he may be a son of God, and disheartened so that he can not be used of God. Do you know there is no place in the Scriptures where it is recorded that God ever used even a discouraged man. Some years ago, in my work I was quite discouraged, and I was ready to hang my harp on the willow. I was very much cast down and depressed. I had been for weeks in that state, when one Monday morning a friend, who had a very large Bible class, came into my study. I used to examine the notes of his Sunday-school lessons, which were equal to a sermon, and he came to me this morning and said, "Well, what did you preach about yesterday?" and I told him. I said, "What did you preach about?" and he said that he preached about Noah. "Did you ever preach about Noah?" "No, I never preached about Noah." "Did you ever study his character?" "No, I never studied his life particularly." "Well," says he, "he is a most wonderful character. It will do you good. You ought to study up that character." When he went out, I took down my Bible, and read about Noah; and then it came over me that Noah worked 120 years and never had a convert, and yet he did not get discouraged; and I said, "Well, I ought not to be discouraged," and I closed my Bible, got up and walked down town, and the cloud had gone. I went down to the noon prayer-meeting, and heard of a little town in the country where they had taken into the church 100 young converts; and I said to myself, I wonder what Noah would have given if he could have heard that; and yet he worked 120 years and didn't get discouraged. And then a man right across the aisle got up and said, "My friends, I wish you to pray for me; I think I'm lost;" and I thought to myself, "I wonder what Noah would have given to hear that." He never heard a man say, "I wish you to pray for me; I think I am lost," and yet he didn't get discouraged! Oh, children of God, let us not get discouraged; let us ask God to forgive us, if we have been discouraged and cast down; let us ask God to give us hope, that we may be ever hopeful. It does me good sometimes to meet some people and take hold of their hands; they are so hopeful, while other people throw a gloom over me because they are all the time cast down, and looking at the dark side, and looking at the obstacles and difficulties that are in the way.

THE BOON OF LIBERTY.

The next thing the Spirit of God does is to give us liberty. He first imparts love; He next inspires hope, and then gives liberty, and that is about the last thing we have in a good many of our churches at the present day. And I am sorry to say there must be a funeral in a good many churches before there is much work done, we shall have to bury the formalism so deep that it will never have any resurrection. The last thing to be found in many a church is liberty.

If the Gospel happens to be preached, the people criticise, as they would a theatrical performance. It is exactly the same, and many a professed Christian never thinks of listening to what the man of God has to say. It is hard work to preach to carnally-minded critics, but "Where the spirit of the Lord is, there is liberty."

Very often a woman will hear a hundred good things in a sermon, and there may be one thing that strikes her as a little out of place, and she will go home and sit down to the table and talk right out before her children and magnify that one wrong thing, and not say a word about the hundred good things that were said. That is what people do who criticise.

God does not use men in captivity. The condition of many is like Lazarus when he came out of the sepulcher bound hand and foot. The bandage was not taken off his mouth, and he could not speak. He had life, and if you had said Lazarus was not alive, you would have told a falsehood, because he was raised from the dead. There are a great many people, the moment you talk to them and insinuate they are not doing what they might, they say: "I have life. I am a Christian." Well, you can't deny it, but they are bound hand and foot.

May God snap these fetters and set His children free, that they may have liberty. I believe He comes to set us free, and wants us to work for Him, and speak for

Him. How many people would like to get up in a social prayer-meeting to say a few words for Christ, but there is such a cold spirit of criticism in the Church that they dare not do it. They have not the liberty to do it. If they get up, they are so frightened with these critics that they begin to tremble and sit down. They can not say anything. Now, that is all wrong. The Spirit of God comes just to give liberty, and wherever you see the Lord's work going on, you will see that Spirit of liberty. People won't be afraid of speaking to one another. And when the meeting is over they will not get their hats and see how quick they can get out of the church, but will begin to shake hands with one another, and there will be liberty there. A good many go to the prayer-meeting out of a mere cold sense of duty. They think "I must attend because I feel it is my duty." They don't think it is a glorious privilege to meet and pray, and to be strengthened, and to help some one else in the wilderness journey.

What we need to-day is love in our hearts. Don't we want it? Don't we want hope in our lives? Don't we want to be hopeful? Don't we want liberty? Now, all this is the work of the Spirit of God, and let us pray God daily to give us love, and hope, and liberty. We read in Hebrews, "Having, therefore, brethren, boldness to enter into the holiest by the blood of Jesus." If you will turn to the passage and read the margin—it says: "Having, therefore, brethren, liberty to enter into the holiest." We can go into the holiest, having freedom of access, and plead for this love and liberty and glorious hope, that we may not rest until God gives us the power to work for Him.

If I know my own heart to-day, I would rather die than live as I once did, a mere nominal Christian, and not used by God in building up His kingdom. It seems a poor empty life to live for the sake of self.

Let us seek to be useful. Let us seek to be vessels meet for the Master's use, that God, the Holy Spirit, may shine fully through us.

> " Know, my soul, thy full salvation;
>   Rise o'er sin, and fear, and care;
> Joy to find, in every station,
>   Something still to do or bear.
>
> " Think what Spirit dwells within thee;
>   Think what Father's smiles are thine;
> Think that Jesus died to win thee:
>   Child of heaven, canst thou repine?
>
> " Haste thee on from grace to glory,
>   Armed by faith, and winged by prayer,
> Heaven's eternal day 's before thee:
>   God's own hand shall guide thee there.
>
> " Soon shall close thy earthly mission,
>   Soon shall pass thy pilgrim days,
> Hope shall change to glad fruition,
>   Faith to sight, and prayer to praise."

"I am so weak, dear Lord! I can not stand
    One moment without Thee;
  But oh, the tenderness of Thy enfolding,
  And oh, the faithfulness of Thine upholding,
And oh, the strength of Thy right hand!
    That strength is enough for me.

" I am so needy, Lord! and yet I know
    All fullness dwells in Thee;
  And hour by hour that never-failing treasure
  Supplies and fills in overflowing measure
My last and greatest need. And so
    Thy grace is enough for me.

" It is so sweet to trust Thy word alone!
    I do not ask to see
  The unveiling of Thy purpose, or the shining
  Of future light on mysteries untwining;
Thy promise-roll is all my own—
    Thy word is enough for me.

" There were strange soul-depths, restless, vast, and broad
    Unfathomed as the sea,
  An infinite craving for some infinite stilling;
  But now Thy perfect love is perfect filling!
Lord Jesus Christ, my Lord, my God,
    Thou, Thou art enough for me! "

CHAPTER II.

POWER "IN" AND "UPON."

You remember that strange, half-involuntary "forty years" of Moses in the "wilderness" of Midian, when he had fled from Egypt. You remember, too, the almost equally strange years of retirement in "Arabia" by Paul, when, if ever, humanly speaking, instant action was needed. And pre eminently you remember the amazing charge of the ascending Lord to the disciples, "Tarry at Jerusalem." Speaking after the manner of men, one could not have wondered if out-spoken Peter, or fervid James, had said: "Tarry, Lord! How long?" "Tarry, Lord! is there not a perishing world, groaning for the 'good news?'" "Tarry! did we hear Thee aright, Lord? Was the word not haste?" Nay; "Being assembled together with them, He commanded them that they should not depart from Jerusalem, but wait for the promise of the Father." (Acts 1: 4.)—*Grosart.*

POWER—"IN" AND "UPON."

The Holy Spirit dwelling in us, is one thing; I think this is clearly brought out in Scripture; and the Holy Spirit upon us for service, is another thing. Now there are only three places we find in Scripture that are dwelling-places for the Holy Ghost.

In the 40th chapter of Exodus, commencing with the 33d verse, are these words:

"And he (that is Moses) reared up the court round about the tabernacle and the altar, and set up the hanging of the court gate. So Moses finished the work.

"Then a cloud covered the tent of the congregation, and the glory of the Lord filled the tabernacle.

"And Moses was not able to enter into the tent of the congregation, because the cloud abode thereon, and the glory of the Lord filled the tabernacle."

The moment that Moses finished the work, the moment that the tabernacle was ready, the cloud came, the Shekinah glory came and filled it so that Moses was not able to stand before the presence of the Lord. I believe firmly, that the moment our hearts are emptied of pride and selfishness and ambition and self-seeking, and everything that is contrary to God's law, the Holy Ghost will come and fill every corner of our hearts; but if we are full of pride and conceit, and ambition and self-seeking, and pleasure and the world, there is no room for the Spirit of God; and I believe many a man is praying to God to fill him when he is full already with something else. Before we pray that God would fill us, I believe we ought to pray Him to empty us.

There must be an emptying before there can be a filling; and when the heart is turned upside down, and everything is turned out that is contrary to God, then the Spirit will come, just as He did in the tabernacle, and fill us with His glory. We read in 2d Chronicles, 5th chapter and 13th verse: "It came even to pass, as the trumpeters and singers were as one to make one sound, to be heard in praising and thanking the Lord, and when they lifted up their voice with the trumpets and cymbals and instruments of music, and praised the Lord, saying, For He is good; for His mercy endureth forever; that then the house was filled with a cloud, even the house of the Lord. So that the priests could not stand to minister by reason of the cloud, for the glory of the Lord had filled the house of God."

PRAISING WITH ONE HEART.

We find, the very moment that Solomon completed the Temple, when all was finished, they were just praising God with one heart—the choristers and the singers and the ministers were all one; there was not any discord; they were all praising God, and the glory of God came and just filled the Temple as the Tabernacle. Now, as you turn over into the New Testament, you will find, instead of coming to Tabernacles and Temples, believers are now the Temple of the Holy Ghost. When, on the day of Pentecost, before

POWER—"IN" AND "UPON."

Peter preached that memorable sermon, as they were praying, the Holy Ghost came, and came in mighty power. We now pray for the Spirit of God to come, and we sing:

> "Come, Holy Spirit, heavenly dove,
> With all thy quickening power;
> Kindle a flame of heavenly love
> In these cold hearts of ours."

I believe, if we understand it, it is perfectly right; but if we are praying for Him to come out of heaven down to earth again, that is wrong, because He is already here; He has not been out of this earth for 1800 years; He has been in the Church, and He is with all believers; the believers in the Church are the called-out ones; they are called out from the world, and every true believer is a Temple for the Holy Ghost to dwell in. In the 14th chapter of John, 17th verse, we have the words of Jesus:

"The Spirit of Truth, whom the world can not receive, because it seeth Him not, neither knoweth Him; but ye know Him, for He dwelleth in you."

"Greater is He that is in you than He that is in the world." If we have the Spirit dwelling in us, He gives us power over the flesh and the world, and over every enemy. "He is dwelling with you, and shall be in you."

Read 1st Corinthians iii, 16: "Know ye not that ye are the temple of God, and that the Spirit of God dwelleth in you?"

There were some men burying an aged saint some time ago, and he was very poor, like many of God's people, poor in this world, but they are very rich, they have all the riches on the other side of life—they have them laid up there where thieves can not get them, and where sharpers can not take them away from them, and where moth can not corrupt—so this aged man was very rich in the other world, and they were just hastening him off to the grave, wanting to get rid of him, when an old minister, who was officiating at the grave, said, "Tread softly, for you are carrying the temple of the Holy Ghost." Whenever you see a believer, you see a temple of the Holy Ghost.

In 1 Cor. vi, 19, 20, we read again: "Know ye not that your body is the temple of the Holy Ghost which is in you, which ye have of God, and ye are not your own for ye are bought with a price, therefore glorify God in your body and in your spirit, which are God's." Thus are we taught that there is a divine resident in every child of God.

I think it is clearly taught in the Scripture that every believer has the Holy Ghost dwelling in him. He may be quenching the Spirit of God, and he may not glorify God as he should, but if he is a believer on the Lord Jesus Christ, the Holy Ghost dwells in him. But I want to call your attention to another fact. I believe to-day, that though Christian men and women have the Holy Spirit dwelling in them, yet He is not dwelling within them in power; in other words, God has a great many sons and daughters without power.

WHAT IS NEEDED.

Nine-tenths, at least, of the church members never think of speaking for Christ. If they see a man, perhaps a near relative, just going right down to ruin, going rapidly, they never think of speaking to him about his sinful course and of seeking to win him to Christ. Now certainly there must be something wrong. And yet when you talk with them you find they have faith, and you can not say they are not children of God; but they have not the power, they have not the liberty, they have not the love that real disciples of Christ should have. A great many people are thinking that we need new measures, that we need new churches, that we need new organs, and that we need new choirs, and all these new things. That is not what the Church of God needs to-day. It is the old power that the Apostles had; that is what we want, and if we have that in our churches, there will be new life. Then we will have new ministers—the same old ministers renewed with power; filled with the Spirit. I remember when in Chicago many were toiling in the work, and it seemed as though the car of salvation didn't move on, when a minister began to cry out from the very depths of his heart, "Oh, God, put new ministers in every pulpit." On next Monday I heard two or three men stand up and say, "We had a new minister last Sunday —the same old minister, but he had got new power," and I firmly believe that is what we want to-day all over America. We want new ministers in the pulpit and new people in the pews. We want people quickened by the Spirit of God, and the Spirit coming down and taking possession of the children of God and giving them power.

Then a man filled with the Spirit will know how to use "the sword of the Spirit." If a man is not filled with the Spirit, he will never know now to use the Book. We are told that this is the sword of the Spirit; and what is an army good for that does not know how to use its weapons? Suppose a battle going on, and I were a general and had a hundred thousand men, great, able-bodied men, full of life, but they could not one of them handle a sword, and not one of them knew how to use his rifle, what would that army be good for? Why, one thousand well-drilled men, with good weapons, would rout the whole of them. The reason why the Church can not overcome the enemy is, because she don't know how to use the sword of the Spirit. People will get up and try to fight the devil with their experiences, but he don't care for that, he will overcome them every time. People are trying to fight the devil with theories and pet ideas, but he will get the victory over them likewise. What we want is to draw the sword of the Spirit. It is that which cuts deeper than anything else.

Turn in your Bibles to Eph. vi, 14: "Stand, therefore, having your loins girt about with truth, and having on the breastplate of righteousness; and your feet shod with the preparation of the gospel of peace; above all (or over all), taking the shield of faith, wherewith ye shall be able to quench all the fiery darts of the wicked. And take the helmet of salvation and the sword of the Spirit, which is the Word of God."

THE GREATEST WEAPON.

The sword of the Spirit is the Word of God, and what we need specially is to be filled with the Spirit, so we shall know how to use the Word. There was a Christian man talking to a skeptic, who was using the Word, and the skeptic said, "I don't believe, sir, in that Book." But the man went right on and he gave him more of the Word; and the man again remarked, "I don't believe the Word," but he kept giving him more, and at last the man was reached. And the brother added, "When I have proved a good sword which does the work of execution, I would just keep right on using it." That is what we want. Skeptics and infidels may say they don't believe in it. It is not our work to make them believe in it; that is the work of the Spirit. Our work is to give them the Word of God; not to preach our theories and our ideas about it, but just to deliver the message as God gives it to us. We read in the Scriptures of the sword of the Lord and Gideon. Suppose Gideon had gone out without the Word, he would have been defeated. But the Lord used Gideon; and I think you find all through the Scriptures, God takes up and uses human instruments. You can not find, I believe, a case in the Bible where a man is converted without God calling in some human agency—using some human instrument; not but what He can do it in His independent sovereignty; there is no doubt about that. Even when by the revealed glory of the Lord Jesus, Saul of Tarsus was smitten to the earth, Annanias was used to open his eyes and lead him into the light of the Gospel. I heard a man once say, if you put a man on a mountain peak, higher than one of the Alpine peaks, God could save him without a human messenger; but that is not His way; that is not His method; but it is "the sword of the Lord and Gideon"; and the Lord and Gideon will do the work; and if we are just willing to let the Lord use us, He will.

"NONE OF SELF."

Then you will find all through the Scriptures, when men were filled with the Holy Spirit, they preached Christ and not themselves. They preached Christ and Him crucified. It says in the first chapter of Luke, 67th verse, speaking of Zacharias, the father of John the Baptist:

"And his father, Zacharias, was filled with the Holy Ghost, and prophesied, saying: Blessed be the Lord God of Israel, for He hath visited and redeemed His people, and hath raised up an horn of salvation for us in the house of His servant David. As He spake by the mouth of His Holy prophets, which have been since the world began."

See, he is talking about the Word. If a man is filled with the Spirit, he will magnify the Word; he will preach the Word, and not himself; he will give this lost world the Word of the living God. "And thou, child, shalt be called the prophet of the Highest; for thou shalt go before the face of the Lord to prepare His ways. To give knowledge of salvation unto His people by the remission of their sins, through the tender mercy of our God, whereby the day-spring from on high hath visited us. To give light to them that sit in darkness and in the shadow of death, to guide our feet into the way of peace. And the child grew and waxed strong in spirit, and was in the deserts till the day of his showing unto Israel." And so we find again that when Elizabeth and Mary met, they talked of the Scriptures, and they were both filled with the Holy Ghost, and at once began to talk of their Lord.

We also find that Simeon, as he came into the temple and found the young child Jesus there, at once began to quote the Scriptures, for the Spirit was upon him. And when Peter stood up on the day of Pentecost, and preached that wonderful sermon, it is said he was filled with the Holy Ghost, and began to preach the Word to the multitude, and it was the Word that cut them. It was the sword of the Lord and Peter, the same as it was the sword of the Lord and Gideon. And we find it says of Stephen, "They were not able to resist the spirit and wisdom by which he spake." Why? Because he gave them the Word of God. And we are told that the Holy Ghost came on Stephen, and none could resist his word. And we read, too, that Paul was full of the Holy Spirit, and that he preached Christ and Him crucified, and that many people were added to the Church. Barnabas was full of faith and the Holy Ghost; and if you will just read and find out what he preached, you will find it was the Word, and many were added to the Lord. So that when a man is full of the Spirit, he begins to preach, not himself, but Christ, as revealed in the Holy Scriptures.

The disciples of Jesus were all filled with the Spirit, and the Word was published; and when the Spirit of God comes down upon the Church, and we are anointed, the Word will be published in the streets, in the lanes, and in the alleys; there will not be a dark cellar nor a dark attic, nor a home where the Gospel will not be carried by some loving heart, if the Spirit comes upon God's people in demonstration and in power.

Library of Davidson College

SPIRITUAL IRRIGATION.

It is possible a man may just barely have life and be satisfied; and I think that a great many are in that condition. In the 3d chapter of John we find that Nicodemus came to Christ and that he received life. At first this life was feeble. You don't hear of him standing up confessing Christ boldly, and of the Spirit coming upon him in great power, though possessing life through faith in Christ. And then turn to the 4th chapter of John, and you will find it speaks of the woman coming to the well of Samaria, and Christ held out the cup of salvation to her and she took it and drank, and it became in her "a well of water springing up into everlasting life." That is better than in the 3d chapter of John; here it came down in a flood into her soul; as some one has said, it came down from the throne of God, and like a mighty current carried her back to the throne of God. Water always rises to its level, and if we get the soul filled with water from the throne of God it will bear us upward to its source.

But if you want to get the best class of Christian life portrayed, turn to the 7th chapter and you will find that it says he that receiveth the Spirit, through trusting in the Lord Jesus, "out of him shall flow rivers of living water." Now there are two ways of digging a well. I remember, when a boy, upon a farm, in New England, they had a well, and they put in an old wooden pump, and I used to have to pump the water from that well upon wash-day, and to water the cattle; and I had to pump and pump and pump until my arm got tired, many a time. But they have a better way now; they don't dig down a few feet and brick up the hole and put the pump in, but they go down through the clay and the sand and the rock, and on down until they strike what they call a lower stream, and then it becomes an artesian well, which needs no labor, as the water rises spontaneously from the depths beneath.

Now I think God wants all His children to be a sort of artesian well; not to keep pumping, but to flow right out. Why, haven't you seen ministers in the pulpit just pumping, and pumping and pumping? I have, many a time, and I have had to do it, too. I know how it is. They stand in the pulpit and talk and talk and talk, and the people go to sleep, they can't arouse them. What is the trouble? Why, the living water is not there; they are just pumping when there is no water in the well. You can't get water out of a dry well; you have to get something in the well, or you can't get anything out. I have seen these wooden pumps where you had to pour water into them before you could pump any water out, and so it is with a good many people; you have to get something in them before you can get anything out. People wonder why it is that they have no Spiritual power. They stand up and talk in meeting, and don't say anything; they say they haven't anything to say, and you find it out soon enough; they need not state it; but they just talk, because they feel it is a duty, and say nothing.

Now I tell you when the Spirit of God is on us for service, resting upon us, we are anointed, and then we can do great things. "I will pour water on him that is thirsty," says God. O, blessed thought—"He that hungers and thirsts after righteousness shall be filled!"

OUTFLOWING STREAMS.

I would like to see some one just full of living water; so full that they couldn't contain it; that they would have to go out and publish the Gospel of the grace of God. When a man gets so full that he can't hold any more, then he is just ready for God's service.

When preaching in Chicago, Dr. Gibson remarked in the inquiry meeting, "Now, how can we find out who is thirsty?" Said he, "I was just thinking how we could find out. If a boy should come down the aisle, bringing a good pail full of clear water, and a dipper, we would soon find out who was thirsty; we would see thirsty men and women reach out for water; but if you should walk down the aisle with an empty bucket, you wouldn't find it out. People would look in and see that there was no water, and say nothing." So said he, "I think that is the reason we are not more blessed in our ministry; we are carrying around empty buckets, and the people see that we have not anything in them, and they don't come forward." I think that there is a good deal of truth in that. People see that we are carrying around empty buckets, and they will not come to us until they are filled. They see we haven't any more than they have. We must have the Spirit of God resting upon us, and then we will have something that gives the victory over the world, the flesh, and the devil; something that gives the victory over our tempers, over our conceits, and over every other evil, and when we can trample these sins under our feet, then people will come to us and say, "How did you get it? I need this power; you have something that I haven't got; I want it." O, may God show us this truth. Have we been toiling all night? let us throw the net on the right side; let us ask God to forgive our sins, and anoint us with power from on high. But remember, He is not going to give this power to an impatient man; He is not going to give it to a selfish man; He will never give it to an ambitious man whose aim is selfish, till first emptied of self; emptied of pride and of all worldly thoughts. Let it be God's glory and not our own that we seek, and when we get to that point, how speedily the Lord will bless us for good. Then will the measure of our blessing be full. Do you know what heaven's measure is? Good measure, pressed down, shaken together, and running over. If we get our heart filled with the Word of God, how is Satan going to get in? How is the world going to get in, for heaven's measure is good measure, full measure, running over. Have you this fullness? If you have not, then seek it; say by the grace of God you will have it, for it is the Father's good pleasure to give us these things. He wants us to shine down in this world; He wants to lift us up for His work; He wants us to have the power to testify for His Son. He has left us in this world to testify for Him. What did He leave us for? Not to buy and sell and to get gain, but to glorify Christ. How are you going to do it without the Spirit? That is the question. How are you to do it without the power of God?

WHY SOME FAIL.

We read in John xx, 22: "And when He had said this, He breathed on them, and saith unto them, Receive ye the Holy Ghost."

Then see Luke xxiv, 49: "And, behold, I send the promise of my Father upon you; but tarry ye in the city of Jerusalem until ye be endued with power from on high."

The first passage tells us He had raised those pierced and wounded hands over them and breathed upon them and said, "Receive ye the Holy Ghost." And I haven't a doubt they received it then, but not in such mighty power as afterward when qualified for their work. It was not in fullness that He gave it to them then, but if they had been like a good many now, they would have said, "I have enough now; I am not going to tarry; I am going to work."

Some people seem to think they are losing time if they wait on God for His power, and so away they go and work without unction; they are working without any anointing, they are working without any power. But after Jesus had said "Receive ye the Holy Ghost," and had breathed on them, He said: "Now you tarry in Jerusalem until you be endued with power from on high." Read in the 1st chapter of Acts, 8th verse: "But ye shall receive power, after that the Holy Ghost is come upon you."

Now, the Spirit had been given them certainly or they could not have believed, and they could not have taken their stand for God and gone through what they did, and endured the scoffs and frowns of their friends, if they had not been converted by the power of the Holy Ghost. But now just see what Christ said:

"Ye shall receive power after that the Holy Ghost is come upon you; and ye shall be witnesses unto me both in Jerusalem and in all Judea, and in Samaria, and unto the uttermost parts of the earth."

Then, the Holy Spirit IN us is one thing, and the Holy Spirit ON us is another; and if these Christians had gone out and went right to preaching then and there, without the power, do you think that scene would have taken place on the day of Pentecost? Don't you think that Peter would have stood up there and beat against the air, while these Jews would have gnashed their teeth and mocked him? But they tarried in Jerusalem; they waited ten days. What! you say. What, the world perishing and men dying! Shall I wait? Do what God tells you. There is no use in running before you are sent; there is no use in attempting to do God's work without God's power. A man working without this unction, a man working without this anointing, a man working without the Holy Ghost upon him, is losing his time after all. So we are not going to lose anything if we tarry till we get this power. That is the object of true service, to wait on God, to tarry till we receive this power for witness-bearing. Then we find that on the day of Pentecost, ten days after Jesus Christ was glorified, the Holy Spirit descended in power. Do you think that Peter and James and John and those apostles doubted it from that very hour? They never doubted it. Perhaps some question the possibility of having the power of God now, and that the Holy Spirit never came afterward in similar manifestation, and will never come again in such power.

FRESH SUPPLIES.

Turn to Acts iv, 31, and you will find He came a second time, and at a place where they were, so that the earth was shaken, and they were filled with this power. The fact is, we are leaky vessels, and we have to keep right under the fountain all the time to keep full of Christ, and so have a fresh supply.

I believe this is a mistake a great many of us are making; we are trying to do God's work with the grace God gave us ten years ago. We say, if it is necessary, we will go on with the same grace. Now, what we want is a fresh supply, a fresh anointing and fresh power, and if we seek it, and seek it with all our hearts, we will obtain it. The early converts were taught to look for that power. Philip went to Samaria, and news reached Jerusalem that there was a great work being done in Samaria, and many converts; and John and Peter went down, and they laid their hands on them, and they received the Holy Ghost for service. I think that is what we Christians ought to be looking for—the Spirit of God for service—that God may use us mightily in the building up of His Church and hastening His glory. In Acts xix we read of twelve men at Ephesus, who, when the inquiry was made if they had received the Holy Ghost since they believed, answered: "We have not so much as heard whether there be any Holy Ghost." I venture to say there are very many, who, if you were to ask them, "Have you received the Holy Ghost since you believed?" would reply, "I don't know what you mean by that." They would be like the twelve men down at Ephesus, who had never understood the peculiar relation of the Spirit to the sons of God in this dispensation. I firmly believe that the Church has just laid this knowledge aside, mislaid it somewhere, and so Christians are without power. Sometimes you can take one hundred members into the Church, and they don't add to its power. Now that is all wrong. If they were only anointed by the Spirit of God, there would be great power if one hundred saved ones were added to the Church.

GREEN FIELDS.

When I was out in California, the first time I went down from the Sierra Nevada Mountains and dropped into the Valley of the Sacramento, I was surprised to find on one farm that everything about it was green—all the trees and flowers, everything was blooming, and everything was green and beautiful, and just across the hedge everything was dried up, and there was not a green thing there, and I could not understand it; I made inquiries, and I found that the man that had everything green, irrigated; he just poured the water right on, and he kept everything green, while the fields that were next to his were as dry as Gideon's fleece without a drop of dew; and so it is with a great many in the Church to-day. They are like these farms in California—a dreary desert, everything parched and desolate, and apparently no life in them. They can sit next to a man who is full of the Spirit of God, who is like a green bay tree, and who is bringing forth fruit, and yet they will not seek a similar blessing. Well, why this difference? Because God has poured water on him that was thirsty; that is the difference. One has been seeking this anointing, and he has received it; and when we want this above everything else God will surely give it to us.

The great question before us now is, *Do* we want it? I remember when I first went to England and gave a Bible reading, I think about the first that I gave in that country, a great many ministers were there, and I did'nt know anything about English theology, and I was afraid I should run against their creeds, and I was a little hampered, especially on this very subject, about the gift of the Holy Spirit for service. I remember particularly a Christian minister there who had his head bowed on his hand, and I thought the good man was ashamed of everything I was saying, and of course that troubled me. At the close of my address he took his hat and away he went, and then I thought, "Well, I shall never see him again." At the next meeting I looked all around for him and he wasn't there, and at the next meeting I looked again, but he was absent; and I thought my teaching must have given him offense. But a few days after that, at a large noon prayer meeting, a man stood up and his face shone as if he had been up in the mountain with God, and I looked at him, and to my great joy it was this brother. He said he was at that Bible reading, and he heard there was such a thing as having fresh power to preach the Gospel; he said he made up his mind that if that was for him he would have it; he said he went home and looked to the Master, and that he never had such a battle with himself in his life. He asked that God would show him the sinfulness of his heart that he knew nothing about, and he just cried mightily to God that he might be emptied of himself and filled with the Spirit, and he said, "God has answered my prayer." I met him in Edinburgh six months from that date, and he told me he had preached the Gospel every night during that time, that he had not preached one sermon but that some remained for conversation, and that he had engagements four months ahead to preach the Gospel every night in different churches. I think you could have fired a cannon ball right through his church and not hit any one before he got this anointing; but it was not thirty days before the building was full and aisles crowded. He had his bucket filled full of fresh water, and the people found it out and came flocking to him from every quarter. I tell you, you can't get the stream higher than the fountain. What we need very specially is power. There was another man whom I have in my mind, and he said, "I have heart disease, I can't preach more than once a week," so he had a colleague to preach for him and do the visiting. He was an old minister, and he couldn't do any visiting. He had heard of this anointing, and said, "I would like to be anointed for my burial. I would like before I go hence to have just one more privilege to preach the Gospel with power." He prayed that God would fill him with the Spirit, and I met him not long after that, and he said, "I have preached on an average eight times a week, and I have had conversions all along." The Spirit came on him. I don't believe that man broke down at first with hard work, so much as with using the machinery without oil, without lubrication. It is not the hard work breaks down ministers, but it is the toil of working without power. Oh, that God may anoint His people! Not the ministry only, but every disciple. Do not suppose pastors are the only laborers needing it. There is not a mother but needs it in her house to regulate her family, just as much as the minister needs it in the pulpit or the Sunday-school teacher needs it in his Sunday-school. We all need it together, and let us not rest day nor night until we possess it; if that is the uppermost thought in our hearts, God will give it to us if we just hunger and thirst for it, and say, "God helping me, I will not rest until endued with power from on high."

MASTER AND SERVANT.

There is a very sweet story of Elijah and Elisha, and I love to dwell upon it. The time had come for Elijah to be taken up, and he said to Elisha, "You stay here at Gilgal, and I will go up to Bethel." There was a theological seminary there, and some young students, and he wanted to see how they were getting along; but Elisha said, "As the Lord liveth, and thy soul liveth, I will not leave thee." And so Elisha just kept close to Elijah. They came to Bethel, and the sons of the prophets came out and said to Elisha, "Do you know that your master is to be taken away?" And Elisha said, "I know it; but you keep still." Then Elijah said to Elisha, "You remain at Bethel until I go to Jericho." But Elisha said, "As the Lord liveth and my soul liveth, I will not leave thee." "You shall not go without me," says Elisha; and then I can imagine that Elisha just put his arm in that of Elijah, and they walked down together. I can see those two mighty men walking down to Jericho, and when they arrived there, the sons of the prophets came and said to Elisha, "Do you know that your master is to be taken away?" "Hush! keep still," says Elisha, "I know it." And then Elijah said to Elisha, "Tarry here awhile; for the Lord hath sent me to Jordan." But Elisha said, "As the Lord liveth and my soul liveth, I will not leave thee. You shall not go without me." And then Elisha came right close to Elijah, and as they went walking down, I imagine Elisha was after something; when they came to the Jordan, Elijah took off his mantle and struck the waters, and they separated hither and thither, and the two passed through like giants, dry-shod, and fifty sons of the prophets came to look at them and watch them. They didn't know but Elijah would be taken up right in their sight. As they passed over Jordan, Elijah said to Elisha, "Now, what do you want?" He knew he was after something. "What can I do for you. Just make your request known." And he said, "I would like a double portion of thy Spirit." I can imagine now that Elijah had given him a chance to ask; he said to himself, "I will ask for enough." Elisha had a good deal of the Spirit, but, says he, "I want a double portion of thy Spirit." "Well," says Elijah, "if you see me when I am taken up, you shall have it." Do you think you could have enticed Elisha from Elijah at that moment? I can almost see the two arm in arm, walking along, and as they walked, there came along the chariot of fire, and before Elisha knew it, Elijah was caught up, and as he went sweeping towards the throne, the servant cried, "My Father! My Father! The chariot of Israel and the horsemen thereof!" Elisha saw him no more. He picked up Elijah's fallen mantle, and returning with that old mantle of his master's, he came to the Jordan and cried for Elijah's God, and the waters separated hither and thither, and he passed through dry-shod. Then the watching prophets lifted up their voices and said, "The Spirit of Elijah is upon Elisha;" and so it was, a double portion of it.

May the Spirit of Elijah, beloved reader, be upon us. If we seek for it we will have it. Oh, may the God of Elijah answer by fire, and consume the spirit of worldliness in the churches, burn up the dross, and make us whole-hearted Christians. May that Spirit come upon us; let that be our prayer in our family altars and in our closets. Let us cry mightily to God that we may have a double portion of the Holy Spirit, and that we may not rest satisfied with this worldly state of living, but let us, like Sampson, shake ourselves and come out from the world, that we may have the power of God.

CHAPTER III.

WITNESSING IN POWER.

A man may as well hew marble without tools, or paint without colors or instruments, or build without materials, as perform any acceptable service without the graces of the Spirit, which are both the materials and the instruments in the work.—*Alleine.*

If we do not have the Spirit of God, it were better to shut the churches, to nail up the doors, to put a black cross on them, and say, "God have mercy on us!" If you ministers have not the Spirit of God, you had better not preach, and you people had better stay at home. I think I speak not too strongly when I say that a church in the land without the Spirit of God is rather a curse than a blessing. If you have not the Spirit of God, Christian worker, remember that you stand in somebody else's way; you are as a tree bearing no fruit standing where another fruitful tree might grow. This is solemn work; the Holy Spirit or nothing, and worse than nothing. Death and condemnation to a church that is not yearning after the Spirit, and crying and groaning until the Spirit has wrought mightily in her midst. He is here; He has never gone back since He descended at Pentecost. He is often grieved and vexed, for He is peculiarly jealous and sensitive, and the one sin never forgiven has to do with His blessed person; therefore let us be very tender towards Him, walk humbly before Him, wait on Him very earnestly, and resolve that about us there should be nothing knowingly continued which should prevent Him dwelling in us, and being with us henceforth and forever. Brethren, peace be unto you and your spirit!—*Spurgeon.*

WITNESSING IN POWER.

THE subject of witness-bearing in the power of the Holy Ghost is not sufficiently understood by the Church. Until we have more intelligence on this point we are laboring under great disadvantage. Now, if you will take your Bible and turn to the 15th chapter of John and the 26th verse, you will find these words: "But when the Comforter is come, whom I will send unto you from the Father, even the Spirit of Truth, which proceedeth from the Father, He shall testify of me; and ye also shall bear witness, because ye have been with me from the beginning." Here we find what the Spirit is going to do, or what Christ said He would do when He came; namely, that He should testify of Him. And if you will turn over to the second chapter of Acts you will find that when Peter stood up on the day of Pentecost, and testified of what Christ had done, the Holy Spirit came down and bore witness to that fact, and men were convicted by hundreds and by thousands. So then man can not preach effectively of himself. He must have the Spirit of God to give ability, and study God's Word in order to testify according to the mind of the Spirit.

WHAT IS THE TESTIMONY?

If we keep back the Gospel of Christ and do not bring Christ before the people, then the Spirit has not the opportunity to work. But the moment Peter stood up on the day of Pentecost and bore testimony to this one fact, that Christ died for sin, and that He had been raised again, and ascended into heaven—the Spirit came down to bear witness to the Person and Work of Christ.

He came down to bear witness to the fact that Christ was in heaven, and if it was not for the Holy Ghost bearing witness to the preaching of the facts of the Gospel, do you think that the Church would have lived during these last eighteen centuries? Do you believe that Christ's death, resurrection and ascension would not have been forgotten as soon as His birth, if it had not been for the fact that the Holy Spirit had come? Because it is very clear, that when John made his appearance on the borders of the wilderness, they had forgotten all about the birth of Jesus Christ. Just thirty short years. It was all gone. They had forgotten the story of the Shepherds; they had forgotten the wonderful scene that took place in the temple, when the Son of God was brought into the temple and the older prophets and prophetesses were there; they had forgotten about the wise men coming to Jerusalem to inquire where He was that was born King of the Jews. That story of His birth seemed to have just faded away; they had forgotten all about it, and when John made his appearance on the borders of the wilderness it was brought back to their minds. And if it had not been for the Holy Ghost coming down to bear witness to Christ, to testify of His death and resurrection, these facts would have been forgotten as soon as His birth.

GREATER WORK.

The witness of the Spirit is the witness of power. Jesus said, "The works that I do shall ye do also, and greater works than these shall ye do because I go to the Father." I used to stumble over that. I didn't understand it. I thought, what greater work could any man do than Christ had done? How could any one raise a dead man who had been laid away in the sepulcher for days, and who had already begun to turn back to dust; how with a word could he call him forth? But the longer I live the more I am convinced it is a greater thing to influence a man's will; a man whose will is set against God; to have that will broken and brought into subjection to God's will—or, in other words, it is a greater thing to have power over a living, sinning, God-hating man, than to quicken the dead. He who could create a world could speak a dead soul into life; but I think the greatest miracle this world has ever seen was the miracle at Pentecost. Here were men who surrounded the Apostles, full of prejudice, full of malice, full of bitterness, their hands, as it were, dripping with the blood of the Son of God, and yet an unlettered man, a man whom they detested, a man whom they hated, stands up there and preaches the Gospel, and three thousand of them are immediately convicted and converted, and become disciples of the Lord Jesus Christ, and are willing to lay down their lives for the Son of God. It may have been on that occasion that Stephen was converted, the first martyr, and some of the men who soon after gave up their lives for Christ.

This seems to me the greatest miracle this world has ever seen. But Peter did not labor alone; the Spirit of God was with him; hence the marvelous results.

The Jewish law required that there should be two witnesses, and so we find that when Peter preached there was a second witness. Peter testified of Christ, and Christ says when the Holy Spirit comes He will testify of Me. And they both bore witness to the verities of our Lord's incarnation, ministry, death, and resurrection, and the result was that a multitude turned as with one heart unto the Lord. Our failure now is, that preachers ignore the Cross, and veil Christ with sapless sermons and superfine language. They don't just present Him to the people plainly, and that is why, I believe, that the Spirit of God don't work with power in our churches. What we need is to preach Christ and present Him to a perishing world. The world can get on very well without you and me, but the world can not get on without Christ, and therefore we must testify of Him, and the world, I believe, to-day is just hungering and thirsting for this divine, satisfying portion. Thousands and thousands are sitting in darkness, knowing not of this great Light, but when we begin to preach Christ honestly, faithfully, sincerely and truthfully; holding Him up, not ourselves; exalting Christ and not our theories; presenting Christ and not our opinions; advocating Christ and not some false doctrine; then the Holy Ghost will come and bear witness. He will testify that what we say is true. When He comes He will confirm the Word with signs following. This is one of the strongest proofs that our Gospel is Divine; that it is of Divine origin; that not only did Christ teach these things, but when leaving the world He said, "He shall glorify Me," and "He will testify of Me." If you will just look at the second chapter of Acts—to that wonderful sermon that Peter preached—the thirty-sixth verse, you read these words: "Therefore let all the house of Israel know assuredly that God hath made that same Jesus whom ye crucified, both Lord and Christ." And when Peter said this the Holy Ghost descended upon the people and testified of Christ—bore witness in signal demonstration that all this was true. And again, in the fortieth verse, "And with many other words did He testify and exhort, saying, Save yourselves from this untoward generation." With many other words did He testify, not only these words that have been recorded, but many other words.

THE SURE GUIDE.

Turn to the sixteenth chapter of John, in the thirteenth verse, and read: "Howbeit, when He, the Spirit of Truth is come, He will guide you into all truth; for He shall not speak of Himself; but whatsoever He shall hear that shall He speak; and He will show you things to come." He will guide you into all truth. Now there is not a truth that we ought to know but the Spirit of God will guide us into it if we will let Him; if we will yield ourselves up to be directed by the Spirit, and let Him lead us, He will guide us into all truth. It would have saved us from a great many dark hours if we had only been willing to let the Spirit of God be our counsellor and guide.

Lot never would have gone to Sodom if he had been guided by the Spirit of God. David never would have fallen into sin and had all that trouble with his family if he had been guided by the Spirit of God.

There are many Lots and Davids now-a-day. The churches are full of them. Men and women are in total darkness, because they have not been willing to be guided by the Spirit of God. "He shall guide you into all truth. He shall not speak of Himself." He shall speak of the ascended glorified Christ.

What would be thought of a messenger, entrusted by an absent husband with a message for his wife or mother who, on arrival, only talked of himself, and his conceits, and ignored both the husband and the message? You would simply call it outrageous. What then must be the crime of the professed teacher who speaks of himself, or some insipid theory, leaving out Christ and His Gospel? If we witness according to the Spirit, we must witness of Jesus.

The Holy Spirit is down here in this dark world to just speak of the Absent One, and He takes the things of Christ and brings them to our mind. He testifies of Christ; He guides us into the truth about Him.

RAPPINGS IN THE DARK.

I want to say right here, that I think in this day a great many children of God are turning aside and committing a grievous sin. I don't know as they think it is a sin, but if we examine the Scriptures, I am sure we will find that it is a great sin. We are told that the Comforter is sent into the world to "guide us into all truth," and if He is sent for that purpose, do we need any other guide? Need we hide in the darkness, consulting with mediums, who profess to call up the spirits of the dead? Do you know what the Word of God pronounces against that fearful sin? I believe it is one of the greatest sins we have to contend with at the present day. It is dishonoring to the Holy Spirit for me to go and summon up the dead and confer with them, even if it were possible.

I would like you to notice the 10th chapter of 1st Chronicles, and 13th verse: "So Saul died for his transgression which he had committed against the Lord, even against the Word of the Lord, which he kept not, and also for asking counsel of one that had a familiar spirit, to inquire of it; and inquired not of the Lord: therefore He slew him, and turned the kingdom unto David the son of Jesse."

God slew him for this very sin. Of the two sins that are brought against Saul here, one is that he would not listen to the Word of God, and the second is that he consulted a familiar spirit. He was snared by this great evil, and sinned against God.

Saul fell right here, and there are a great many of God's professed children to-day who think there is no harm in consulting a medium who pretends to call up some of the departed to inquire of them.

But how dishonoring it is to God who has sent the Holy Spirit into this world to guide us "into all truth." There is not a thing that I need to know, there is not a thing that is important for me to know; there is not a thing that I ought to know but the Spirit of God will reveal it to me through the Word of God, and if I turn my back upon the Holy Spirit, I am dishonoring the Spirit of God, and I am committing a grievous sin. You know we read in Luke, where that rich man in the other world wanted to have some one sent to his father's house to warn his five brothers, Christ said They have Moses and the prophets, and if they will not hear them, they will not hear one though he rose from the dead. Moses and the prophets, the part of the Bible then completed, that is enough. But a great many people now want something besides the Word of God, and are turning aside to these false lights.

SPIRITS THAT PEEP AND MUTTER.

There is another passage which reads, "And when they shall say unto you, seek unto them that have familiar spirits, and unto wizards that peep and mutter: Should not a people seek unto their God? for the living to the dead?" What is that but table-rapping, and cabinet-hiding? If it was a message from God, do you think you would have to go into a dark room and put out all the lights? In secret my Master taught nothing. God is not in that movement, and what we want, as children of God, is to keep ourselves from this evil. And then notice the verse following, quoted so often out of its connection. "To the law and to the testimony; if they speak not according to this word, it is because there is no light in them." Any man, any woman, who comes to us with any doctrine that is not according to the law and the testimony, let us understand that they are from the evil one, and that they are enemies of righteousness. They have no light in them. Now you will find these people who are consulting familiar spirits, first and last, attack the Word of God. They don't believe it. Still a great many people say, you must hear both sides— but if a man should write me a most slanderous letter about my wife, I don't think I would have to read it;

I should tear it up and throw it to the winds. Have I to read all the infidel books that are written, to hear both sides? Have I to take up a book that is a slander on my Lord and Master, who has redeemed me with His blood? Ten thousand times No; I will not touch it.

"Now the Spirit speaketh expressly, that in the latter times some shall depart from the faith, giving heed to seducing spirits, and doctrines of devils." 1 Tim., iv, 1. That is pretty plain language, isn't it? "Doctrines of devils." Again, "speaking lies in hypocrisy; having their consciences seared with a hot iron." There are other passages of Scripture warning against every delusion of Satan. Let us ever remember the Spirit has been sent into the world to guide us into all truth. We don't want any other guide; He is enough. Some people say, "Is not conscience a safer guide than the Word and the Spirit?" No, it is not. Some people don't seem to have any conscience, and don't know what it means. Their education has a good deal to do with conscience. There are persons who will say that their conscience did not tell them that they had done wrong until after the wrong was done; but what we want, is something to tell us a thing is wrong before we do it. Very often a man will go and commit some awful crime, and after it is done his conscience will wake up and lash and scourge him, and then it is too late, the act is done.

THE UNERRING GUIDE.

I am told by people who have been over the Alps, that the guide fastens them, if they are going in a dangerous place, right to himself, and he just goes on before; they are fastened to the guide.

And so should the Christian be linked to His unerring Guide, and be safely upheld. Why, if a man was going through the Mammoth Cave, it would be death to him if he strayed away from his guide—if separated from him, he would certainly perish; there are pitfalls in that cave and a bottomless river, and there would be no chance for a man to find his way through that cave without a guide or a light. So there is no chance for us to get through the dark wilderness of this world alone. It is folly for a man or woman to think that they can get through this evil world without the light of God's Word and the guidance of the Divine Spirit. God sent Him to guide us through this great journey, and if we seek to work independent of Him, we shall stumble into the deep darkness of eternity's night.

But bear in mind the *Words* of the Spirit of God; if you want to be guided, you must study the Word; because the Word is the light of the Spirit. In the 14th chapter of John and 26th verse, we read:

"But the Comforter, which is the Holy Ghost, whom the Father will send in my name, He shall teach you all things, and bring all things to your remembrance, whatsoever I have said unto you."

Again in John xvi, 13:

"Howbeit when He, the Spirit of Truth, is come, He will guide you into all truth: for He shall not speak of Himself; but whatsoever He shall hear, that shall He speak: and He will show you things to come."

"He will show you things to come." A great many people seem to think that the Bible is out of date, that it is an old book, and they think it has passed its day. They say it was very good for the dark ages, and that there is some very good history in it; but then it was not intended for the present time; that we are living in a very enlightened age, and that men can get on very well without the old book; that we have outgrown it. They think we have no use for it, because it is an old book. Now you might just as well say that the sun, which has shone so long, is now so old that it is out of date, and that whenever a man builds a house he need not put any windows in it, because we have got a newer light and a better light; we have gaslight and this new electric light. These are something new; and I would advise people, if they think the Bible is too old and worn out, when they build houses, not to put any windows in them, but just to light them with this new electric light; that is something new, and this is what they are anxious for. People talk about this Book as if they understood it; but we don't know much about it yet. The press gives us the daily news of what has taken place. This Bible, however, tells us what is about to take place. This *is* new; we have the news here in this Book; this tells us of the things that will surely come to pass; and that is a great deal newer than anything in the newspapers. It tells us that the Spirit shall teach us all things; not only guide us into all truth, but teach us all things; He teaches us how to pray, and I don't think there has ever been a prayer upon this sin-cursed earth that has been indicted by the Holy Spirit but was answered. There is much praying that is not indicted by the Holy Spirit. In former years I was very ambitious to get rich; I used to pray for one hundred thousand dollars; that was my aim, and I used to say, "God does not answer my prayer; He does not make me rich." But I had no warrant for such a prayer; yet a good many people pray in that way; they think that they pray, but they do not pray according to the Scriptures. The Spirit of God has nothing to do with their prayers, and such prayers are not the product of His teaching.

It is the Spirit who teaches us how to answer our enemies. If a man strikes me, I should not pull out a revolver and shoot him. The Spirit of the Lord don't teach me revenge; He don't teach me that it is necessary to draw the sword and cut a man down in order to defend my rights. Some people say, You are a coward if you don't strike back. Christ says, turn the other cheek to him who smites. I would rather take Christ's teaching than any other. I don't think a man gains much by loading himself down with weapons to defend himself. There has been life enough sacrificed in this country to teach men a lesson in this regard. The Word of God is a much better protection than the revolver. We had better take the Word of God to protect us, by accepting its teaching, and living out its precepts.

AN AID TO MEMORY.

It is a great comfort to us to remember that another office of the Spirit is to bring the teaching of Jesus to our remembrance. This was our Lord's promise, " He shall teach you all things, and bring all things to your remembrance." Jno. xiv, 26.

How striking that is. I think there are many Christians who have had that experience. They have been testifying, and found that while talking for Christ the

Spirit has just brought into mind some of the sayings of the Lord Jesus Christ, and their mind was soon filled with the Word of God. When we have the Spirit resting upon us, we can speak with authority and power, and the Lord will bless our testimony and bless our work. I believe the reason why God makes use of so few in the Church, is because there is not in them the power that God can use. He is not going to use our ideas, but we must have the Word of God hid in our hearts, and then, the Holy Spirit inflaming us, we will have the testimony which will be rich, and sweet, and fresh, and the Lord's Word will vindicate itself in blessed results. God wants to use us; God wants to make us channels of blessing; but we are in such a condition He does not use us. That is the trouble; there are so many men who have no testimony for the Lord; if they speak, they speak without saying anything, and if they pray, their prayer is powerless; they do not plead in prayer; their prayer is just a few set phrases that you have heard too often. Now what we want, is to be so full of the Word, that the Spirit coming upon us shall bring to mind—bring to our remembrance—the words of the Lord Jesus.

In 1 Cor. ii, 9, it is written: "Eye hath not seen, nor ear heard, neither have entered into the heart of man the things which God hath prepared for them that love Him."

We hear that quoted so often in prayer—many a man weaves it into his prayer and stops right there. And the moment you talk about Heaven, they say, "Oh, we don't know anything about Heaven; it hath not entered into the heart of man; eye hath not seen; it is all speculation; we have nothing to do with it; and they say they quote it as it is written." "Eye hath not seen, nor ear heard; neither have entered into the heart of man the things which God hath prepared for them that love Him." What next—"but God hath revealed them unto us by His Spirit." You see the Lord hath revealed them unto us: "For the Spirit searches all things—yea, the deep things of God." That is just what the Spirit does.

LONG AND SHORT SIGHT.

He brings to our mind what God has in store for us. I heard a man, some time ago, speaking about Abraham. He said "Abraham was not tempted by the well-watered plains of Sodom, for Abraham was what you might call a long-sighted man; he had his eyes set on the city which had foundation—'whose Builder and Maker is God.'" But Lot was a short-sighted man; and there are many people in the Church who are very short-sighted; they only see things right around them they think good. Abraham was long-sighted; he had glimpses of the celestial city. Moses was long-sighted, and he left the palaces of Egypt and identified himself with God's people—poor people, who were slaves; but he had something in view yonder; he could see something God had in store. Again there are some people who are sort of long-sighted and short-sighted, too. I have a friend who has one eye that is long-sighted and the other is short-sighted; and I think the Church is full of this kind of people. They want one eye for the world and the other for the Kingdom of God. Therefore, everything is blurred, one eye is long and the other is short, all is confusion, and they "see men as trees walking." The Church is filled with that sort of people. But Stephen was long-sighted; he looked clear into heaven; they couldn't convince him even when he was dying, that Christ had not ascended to heaven. "Look, look yonder," he says, "I see Him over there; He is on the throne, standing at the right hand of God;" and he looked clear into heaven; the world had no temptation for him; he had put the world under his feet. Paul was another of those long-sighted men; he had been caught up and seen things unlawful for him to utter; things grand and glorious. I tell you when the Spirit of God is on us the world looks very empty; the world has a very small hold upon us, and we begin to let go our hold of it. When the Spirit of God is on us we will just let go the things of time and lay hold of things eternal. This is the Church's need to-day; we want the Spirit to come in mighty power, and consume all the vile dross there is in us. Oh! that the Spirit of fire may come down and burn everything in us that is contrary to God's blessed Word and Will.

In John xiv, 16, we read of the Comforter. This is the first time He is spoken of as the Comforter. Christ had been their Comforter. God had sent Him to comfort the sorrowing. It was prophesied of Him, "The Spirit of the Lord is upon me, because He hath anointed me to preach the Gospel to the poor; He has sent me to heal the broken-hearted." You can't heal the broken-hearted without the Comforter; but the world would not have the first Comforter, and so they rose up and took Him to Calvary and put him to death; but on going away He said, "I will send you another Comforter; you shall not be comfortless; be of good cheer, little flock; it is the Father's good pleasure to give you the kingdom." All these sweet passages are brought to the remembrance of God's people, and they help us to rise out of the fog and mist of this world. O, what a comforter is the Holy Spirit of God!

THE FAITHFUL FRIEND.

The Holy Spirit tells a man of his faults in order to lead him to a better life. In John xvi, 8, we read: "He is to reprove the world of sin." Now, there are a class of people who don't like this part of the Spirit's work. Do you know why? Because He convicts *them* of sin; they don't like that. What they want is some one to speak comforting words and make everything pleasant; keep everything all quiet; tell them there is peace when there is war; tell them it is light when it is dark, and tell them everything is growing better; that the world is getting on amazingly in goodness; that it is growing better all the time; that is the kind of preaching they seek for. Men think they are a great deal better than their fathers were. That suits human nature, for it is full of pride. Men will strut around and say, "Yes, I believe that; the world is improving; I am a good deal better man than father was; my father was too strict; he was one of those old Puritanical men who was so rigid. O, we are getting on; we are more liberal; my father wouldn't think of going out riding on Sunday, but we will; we will trample the laws of God under our feet; we are better than our fathers."

That is the kind of preaching which some dearly love,

and there are preachers who tickle such itching ears. When you bring the Word of God to bear upon them, and when the Spirit drives it home, then men will say: "I don't like that kind of preaching; I will never go to hear that man again;" and sometimes they will get up and stamp their way out of church before the speaker gets through; they don't like it. But when the Spirit of God is at work he convicts men of sin. "When He comes He will reprove the world of sin, of righteousness and of judgment; of sin"—not because men swear and lie and steal and get drunk and murder—"of sin because they believe not on Me."

THE CLIMAX SIN.

That is the sin of the world. Why, a great many people think that unbelief is a sort of misfortune, but do not know, if you will allow me the expression, it is the damning sin of the world to-day; that is what unbelief is, the mother of all sin. There would not be a drunkard walking the streets, if it were not for unbelief; there would not be a harlot walking the streets, if it were not for unbelief; there would not be a murderer, if it was not for unbelief; it is the germ of all sin. Don't think for a moment that it is a misfortune, but just bear in mind it is an awful sin, and may the Holy Spirit convict every reader that unbelief is making God a liar. Many a man has been knocked down on the streets because some one has told him he was a liar. Unbelief is giving God the lie; that is the plain English of it. Some people seem to boast of their unbelief; they seem to think it is quite respectable to be an infidel and doubt God's Word, and they will vainly boast and say, "I have intellectual difficulties; I can't believe." Oh that the Spirit of God may come and convict men of sin! That is what we need—His convicting power, and I am so thankful that God has not put that into our hands. We have not to convict men; if we had I would get discouraged, and give up preaching, and go back to business within the next forty-eight hours. It is my work to preach and hold up the Cross and testify of Christ; but it is His work to convict men of sin and lead them to Christ. One thing I have noticed, that some conversions don't amount to anything; that if a man professes to be converted without conviction of sin, he is one of those stony-ground hearers who don't bring forth much fruit. The first little wave of persecution, the first breath of opposition, and the man is back in the world again. Let us pray, dear Christian reader, that God may carry on a deep and thorough work, that men may be convicted of sin so that they can not rest in unbelief. Let us pray God it may be a thorough work in the land. I would a great deal rather see a hundred men thoroughly converted, truly born of God, than to see a thousand professed conversions where the Spirit of God has not convicted of sin. Don't let us cry "Peace, peace, when there is no peace." Don't go to the man who is living in sin, and tell him all he has to do is to stand right up and profess, without any hatred for sin. Let us ask God first to show every man the plague of his own heart, that the Spirit, may convict them of sin. Then will the work in our hands be real, and deep, and abide the fiery trial which will try every man's labor.

Thus far, we have found the work of the Spirit is to impart life, to implant hope, to give liberty, to testify of Christ, to guide us into all truth, to teach us all things, to comfort the believers, and to convict the world of sin.

> "Holy Spirit, faithful guide,
> Ever near the Christian's side;
> Gently lead us by the hand,
> Pilgrims in a desert land;
> Weary souls for e'er rejoice,
> While they hear that sweetest voice,
> Whisp'ring softly, wanderer come!
> Follow Me, I'll guide thee home.
>
> "Ever present, truest Friend,
> Ever near Thine aid to lend,
> Leave us not to doubt and fear,
> Groping on in darkness drear,
> When the storms are raging sore,
> Hearts grow faint, and hopes give o'er;
> Whisp'ring softly, wanderer come!
> Follow Me, I'll guide thee home.
>
> "When our days of toil shall cease,
> Waiting still for sweet release,
> Nothing left but heaven and prayer,
> Wond'ring if our names were there,
> Wading deep the dismal flood,
> Pleading nought but Jesus' blood;
> Whisp'ring softly, wanderer come!
> Follow Me, I'll guide the home.

"Oh! Spirit of God, whose voice I hear,
   Sweeter than sweetest music, appealing
   In tones of tenderness and love;
Whose comforts delight my soul, and
Fills the temple of my heart with joy beyond compare.
I need Thee day by day, and each day's moment, Lord.
I sigh for greater likeness
To Him who loved me unto death, and loves me still.
'Tis Thine to lead me to Him; 'tis Thine to ope the eye,
To manifest His royal glories to my longing heart;
'Tis Thine the slumbering saint to waken
And discipline this blood-touched ear
To hearken to my heavenly Lover's voice,
And quickly speed His summons to obey.
Oh! Spirit of the Mighty God, uplift my faith
Till heaven's precious light shall flood my soul,
And the shining of my face declare
That I have seen the face of God."

CHAPTER IV.

POWER IN OPERATION.

"Ye are not your own." "Your bodies are the temples of the Holy Ghost." Is that an unmeaning metaphor, or an over-worded expression? When the Holy Spirit enters the soul, heaven enters with Him. The heart is compared to a temple. God never enters without His attendants; *repentance* cleanses the house; *faith* provides for the house; *watchfulness*, like the porter, takes care of it; *prayer* is a lively messenger, learns what is wanted, and then goes for it; *faith* tells him where to go, and he never goes in vain; *joy* is the musician of this temple, tuning to the praises of God and the Lamb; and this terrestrial temple shall be removed to the celestial world, for the trumpet shall sound, and the dead shall be raised.—*Rowland Hill.*

POWER IN OPERATION.

THE power we have been considering is the Presence of the Holy Spirit. He is omnipotent. Power in operation is the actions of the Spirit or the fruit of the Spirit. This we shall now consider. Paul writes in Gal. v, 16, etc.:

"This I say then, walk in the Spirit, and ye shall not fulfill the lust of the flesh. For the flesh lusteth against the Spirit, and the Spirit against the flesh; and these are contrary, the one to the other; so that ye can not do the things that ye would. But if ye be led of the Spirit, ye are not under the law." * * * But the fruit of the Spirit is love, joy, peace, long-suffering, gentleness, goodness, faith, meekness, temperance; against such there is no law. And they that are Christ's have crucified the flesh with the affections and lusts. If we live in the Spirit, let us also walk in the Spirit. Let us not be desirous of vainglory, provoking one another, envying one another."

Now there is a life of perfect peace, perfect joy, and perfect love, and that ought to be the aim of every child of God; that ought to be their standard; and they should not rest until having attained to that position. That is God's standard, where He wants all His children. These nine graces mentioned in this chapter in Galatians can be divided in this way: Love and peace and joy are all to God. God looks for that fruit from each one of His children, and that is the kind of fruit which is acceptable with Him. Without that we can not please God. He wants, above everything else that we possess, love, peace and joy. And then the next three—goodness, long-suffering and gentleness—are towards man. That is our outward life to those that we are coming in contact with continually—daily, hourly. The next three—faith, temperance, meekness—are in relation to ourselves; and in that way we can just take the three divisions, and it will be of some help to us.

The first thing that meets us as we enter the kingdom of God, you might say are these first three graces,

LOVE, PEACE, AND JOY.

When a man who has been living in sin turns from his sins, and turns to God with all his heart, he is met on the threshold of the divine life by these sister graces. The love of God is shed abroad in his heart by the Holy Ghost. The peace of God comes at the same time, and also the joy of the Lord. We can all put the test to ourselves, if we have them. It is not anything that we can make. The great trouble with many is that they are trying to make these graces. They are trying to make love; they are trying to make peace; they are trying to make joy. But they are not creatures of human planting. To produce them of ourselves is impossible. That is an act of God. They come from above. It is God who speaks the word and gives the love; it is God who gives the peace; it is God who gives the joy, and we possess all by receiving Jesus Christ by faith into the heart; for when Christ comes by faith into the heart, then the Spirit is there, and if we have the Spirit, we will have the fruit.

If the whole Church of God could live as the Lord would have them live, why Christianity would be the mightiest power this world has ever seen. It is the low standard of Christian life that is causing so much trouble. There are a great many stunted Christians in the Church; their lives are stunted; they are like a tree planted in poor soil—the soil is hard and stony, and the roots can not find the rich loamy soil needed. Such believers have not grown in these sweet graces. Peter, in his second epistle, 1st chapter and 5th verse, writes:

"And besides this, giving all diligence, add to your faith virtue; and to virtue knowledge; and to knowledge temperance; and to temperance patience; and to patience, godliness; and to godliness, brotherly kindness; and to brotherly kindness, charity. For if these things be in you and abound, they make you that ye shall neither be barren nor unfruitful in the knowledge of our Lord Jesus Christ."

Now, if we have these things in us, I believe that we will be constantly bringing forth fruit that will be acceptable with God. It won't be just a little every now and then, when we spur ourselves up and work ourselves up into a certain state of mind or into an excited condition, and work a little while and then become cold, and discouraged, and disheartened, but we shall be neither unfruitful nor barren, bringing forth fruit constantly, we will grow in grace and be filled with the Spirit of God.

WHAT WINS.

A great many parents have inquired of me how to win

their children. They say they have talked with them, and sometimes they have scolded them and have lectured them, and signally failed. I think there is no way so sure to win our families and our neighbors, and those about whom we are anxious, to Christ, than just to adorn the doctrine of Jesus Christ in our lives, and grow in all these graces. If we have peace and joy and love and gentleness and goodness and temperance; not only being temperate in what we drink, but in what we eat, and temperate in our language, guarded in our expressions; if we just live in our homes as the Lord would have us, an even Christian life day by day, we shall have a quiet and silent power proceeding from us, that will constrain them to believe on the Lord Jesus Christ. But an uneven life, hot to-day and cold tomorrow, will only repel. Many are watching God's people. It is just the very worst thing that can happen to those whom we want to win to Christ, to see us, at any time, in a cold, backslidden state. This is not the normal condition of the Church; it is not God's intention; He would have us growing in all these graces, and the only true, happy, Christian life is to be growing, constantly growing in the love and favor of God, growing in all those delightful graces of the Spirit.

Even the vilest, the most impure, acknowledge the power of goodness; they recognize the fruit of the Spirit. It may condemn their lives and cause them to say bitter things at times, but down deep in their hearts they know that the man or woman who is living that kind of life, is superior to them. The world don't satisfy them, and if we can show the world that Jesus Christ does satisfy us in our present life, it will be more powerful than the eloquent words of professional reformers. A man may preach with the eloquence of an angel, but if he don't live what he preaches, and act out in his home and his business what he professes, his testimony goes for naught, and the people say it is all hypocrisy after all; it is all a sham. Words are very empty, if there is nothing back of them. Your testimony is poor and worthless, if there is not a record back of that testimony consistent with what you profess. What we need is to pray to God to lift us up out of this low, cold, formal state that we have been living in, that we may live in the atmosphere of God continually, and that the Lord may lift upon us the light of his countenance, and that we may shine in this world, reflecting His grace and glory.

The first of the graces spoken of in Galatians, and the last mentioned in Peter, is charity or love. We can not serve God, we can not work for God unless we have love. That is the key which unlocks the human heart. If I can prove to a man that I come to him out of pure love; if a mother shows by her actions that it is pure love that prompts her advising her boy to lead a different life, not a selfish love, but that it is for the glory of God, it won't be long before that mother's influence will be felt by that boy, and he will begin to think about this matter, because true love touches the heart quicker than anything else.

POWER OF LOVE.

Love is the badge that Christ gave His disciples. Some put on one sort of badge and some another. Some put on a strange kind of dress, that they may be known as Christians, and some put on a crucifix, or something else, that they may be known as Christians. But love is the only badge by which the disciples of our Lord Jesus Christ are known. "By this shall all men know that ye are My disciples, if ye have love one toward another."

Therefore, though a man stand before an audience and speak with the eloquence of a Demosthenes, or of the greatest living orator, if there is no love back of his words, it is like sounding brass and a tinkling cymbal. I would recommend all Christians to read the thirteenth chapter of First Corinthians constantly, abiding in it day and night, not spending a night or a day there, but just go in there and spend all our time—summer and winter, twelve months in the year, then the power of Christ and Christianity would be felt as it never has been in the history of the world. See what this chapter says:

"Though I speak with the tongues of men and of angels, and have not charity, I am become *as* sounding brass or a tinkling cymbal. And though I have *the gift* of prophecy, and understand all mysteries, and all knowledge; and though I have all faith, so that I could remove mountains, and have not charity, I am nothing."

A great many are praying for faith; they want extraordinary faith; they want remarkable faith. They forget that love exceeds faith. The CHARITY spoken of in the above verses, is LOVE, the fruit of the Spirit, the great motive-power of life. What the Church of God needs to-day is love—more love to God and more love to our fellow-men. If we love God more, we will love our fellow-men more. There is no doubt about that. I used to think that I should like to have lived in the days of the prophets; that I should like to have been one of the prophets, to prophesy, and to see the beauties of heaven and describe them to men; but, as I understand the Scriptures now, I would a good deal rather live in the thirteenth chapter of 1st Corinthians and have this love that Paul is speaking of, the love of God burning in my soul like an unquenchable flame, so that I may reach men and win them for heaven.

A man may have wonderful knowledge, that may unravel the mysteries of the Bible, and yet be as cold as an icicle. He may glisten like the snow in the sun. Sometimes you have wondered why it was that certain ministers who have had such wonderful magnetism, who have such a marvelous command of language, and who preach with such mental strength, haven't had more conversions. I believe, if the truth was known, you would find no divine love back of their words, no pure love in their sermons. You may preach like an angel, Paul says, "with the tongues of men and of angels," but if you have not love, it amounts to nothing. "And though I bestow all my goods to feed the poor,"—a man may be very charitable, and give away all his goods; a man may give all he has, but if it is not the love of God which prompts the gift, it will not be acceptable with God. "And though I give my body to be burned, and have not charity"—have not love—"it profiteth me nothing." A man may go to the stake for his principles; he may go to the stake for what he believes, but if it is not love to God which actuates him, it will not be acceptable to God.

LOVE'S WONDERFUL EFFECTS.

"Charity suffereth long, and is kind; charity envieth not; charity vaunteth not itself, is not puffed up.

"Doth not behave itself unseemly, seeketh not her own, is not easily provoked, thinketh no evil."

That's the work of love. It is not easily provoked. Now if a man has no love of God in his heart, how easy it is to become offended; perhaps with the church because some members of the church don't treat him just right, or some men of the church don't bow to him on the street, he takes offense, and that is the last you see of him. Love is long-suffering. If I love the Lord Jesus Christ, these little things are not going to separate me from His people. They are like the dust in the balance. Nor will the cold, formal treatment of hypocrites in the church quench that love I have in my heart for Him. If this love is in the heart, and the fire is burning on the altar, we will not be all the time finding fault with other people and criticising what they have done.

CRITICS BEWARE.

Love will rebuke evil, but will not rejoice in it. Love will be impatient of sin, but patient with the sinner. To form the habit of finding fault constantly, is very damaging to spiritual life; it is about the lowest and meanest position that a man can take. I never saw a man who was aiming to do the best work, but there could have been some improvement; I never did anything in my life, I never addressed an audience, that I didn't think I could have done better, and I have often upbraided myself that I had not done better; but to sit down and find fault with other people when we are doing nothing ourselves, not lifting our hands to save some one, is all wrong, and is the opposite of holy, patient, divine love.

Love is forbearance; and what we want is to get this spirit of criticism and fault finding out of the Church and out of our hearts; and let each one of us live as if we had to answer for ourselves, and not for the community, at the last day. If we are living according to the 13th chapter of Corinthians, we will not be all the time finding fault with other people. "Love suffereth long, and is kind." Love forgets itself, and don't dwell upon itself. The woman who came to Christ with that alabaster box, I venture to say, never thought of herself. Little did she know what an act she was performing. It was just her love for the Master. She forgot the surroundings, she forgot everything else that was there; she broke that box and poured the ointment upon Him, and filled the house with its odor. The act, as a memorial, has come down these 1800 years. It is right here—the perfume of that box is in the world to-day. That ointment was worth $40 or $50; no small sum of those days for a poor woman. Judas sold the Son of God for about $15 or $20. But what this woman gave to Christ was everything that she had, and she became so occupied with Jesus Christ that she didn't think what people were going to say. So when we act with a single eye for the glory of our Lord, not finding fault with everything about us, but doing what we can in the power of this love, then will our deeds for God speak, and the world will acknowledge that we have been with Jesus, and that this glorious love has been shed abroad in our hearts.

If we don't love the Church of God, I am afraid it

won't do us much good; if we don't love the blessed Bible, it will not do us much good. What we want, then, is to have love for Christ, to have love for His word, and to have love for the Church of God, and when we have love, and are living in that spirit, we will not be in the spirit of finding fault and working mischief.

AFTER LOVE, WHAT?

After love comes peace. I have before remarked, a great many people are trying to make peace. But that has already been done. God has not left it for us to do; all that we have to do is to enter into it. It is a condition, and instead of our trying to make peace and to work for peace, we want to cease all that, and sweetly enter into peace.

If I discover a man in the cellar complaining because there is no light there, and because it is cold and damp, I say: "My friend, come up out of the cellar. There is a good warm sun up here, a beautiful spring day, and it is warm, it is cheerful and light; come up, and enjoy it." Would he reply, "O, no, sir; I am trying to see if I can make light down here; I am trying to work myself into a warm feeling." And there he is working away, and he has been at it for a whole week. I can imagine my reader smile; but you may be smiling at your own picture; for this is the condition of many whom I daily meet who are trying to do this very thing —they are trying to work themselves into peace and joyful feelings. Peace is a condition into which we enter; it is a state; and instead of our trying to make peace, let us believe what God's Word declares, that peace has already been made by the blood of the Cross.

Christ has made peace for us, and now what He desires is that we believe it and enter into it. Now, the only thing that can keep us from peace is sin. God turneth the way of the wicked upside down. There is no peace for the wicked, saith my God. They are like the troubled sea that can not rest, casting up filth and mire all tne while; but peace with God by faith in Jesus Christ—peace through the knowledge of forgiven sin, is like a rock; the waters go dashing and surging past it, but it abides. When we find peace, we shall not find it on the ground of innate goodness; it comes from without ourselves, but into us. In the 16th chapter of John and the 33d verse we read: "These things have I spoken unto you, that in me ye might have peace." In me ye might have peace. Jesus Christ is the author of peace. He procured peace. His gospel is the gospel of peace. "Behold I bring you good tidings of great joy which shall be unto all people; for unto you is born this day in the city of David a Saviour," and then came that chorus from heaven "Glory to God in the highest; peace on earth." He brought peace. "In the world ye shall have tribulation, but be of good cheer, I have overcome the world."

How true that in the world we have tribulation. Are you in tribulation? Are you in trouble? Are you in sorrow? Remember this is our lot. Paul had tribulation, and others shared in grief. Nor shall we be exempt from trial. But within, peace may reign undisturbed. If sorrow is our lot, peace is our legacy. Jesus gives peace; and do you know there is a good deal of difference between His peace and our peace? Any one can disturb our peace, but they can't disturb His peace.

That is the kind of peace He has left us. Nothing can offend those who trust in Christ.

NOT EASILY OFFENDED.

In the 119th Psalm and the 165th verse, we find "Great peace have they who love Thy law; and nothing shall offend them." The study of God's Word will secure peace. You take those Christians who are rooted and grounded in the Word of God, and you find they have great peace; but it is these who don't study their Bible, and don't know their Bible, who are easily offended when some little trouble comes, or some little persecution, and their peace is all disturbed; just a little breath of opposition, and their peace is all gone.

Sometimes I am amazed to see how little it takes to drive all peace and comfort from some people. Some slandering tongue will readily blast it. But if we have the peace of God, the world can not take that from us. It can not give it; it can not destroy it. We have to get it from above the world; it is peace which Christ gives. "Great peace have they which love Thy law, and nothing shall offend them." Christ says "blessed is he, whosoever shall not be offended in Me." Now, if you will notice, wherever there is a Bible-taught Christian, one who has the Bible well marked, and daily feeds upon the Word by prayerful meditation, he will not be easily offended.

Such are the people who are growing and working all the while. But it is these people who never open their Bibles, these people who never study the Scriptures, who become offended, and are wondering why they are having such a hard time. They are the persons who tell you that Christianity is not what it has been recommended to them; that they have found it was not all that we claim it to be. The real trouble is, they have not done as the Lord has told them to do. They have neglected the Word of God. If they had been studying the Word of God, they would not be in that condition. If they had been studying the Word of God, they would not have wandered these years away from God, living on the husks of the world. But the trouble is, they have neglected to care for the new life; they haven't fed it, and the poor soul, being starved, sinks into weakness and decay, and is easily stumbled or offended.

I met a man who confessed his soul had fed on nothing for forty years. "Well," said I, "that is pretty hard for the soul—giving it nothing to feed on!" And that man is but a type of thousands and tens cf thousands to-day; their poor souls are starving. This body that we inhabit for a day, and then leave, we take good care of; we feed it three times a day, and we clothe it, and take care of it, and deck it, and by and by it is going into the grave to be eaten up by the worms; but the inner man, that is to live on and on, and on forever, is lean and starved.

SWEET WORDS.

In the 6th chapter of Numbers and 22d verse we read :

"And the Lord spake unto Moses, saying: Speak unto Aaron and unto his sons, saying, on this wise ye shall bless the children of Israel, saying unto them: The Lord bless thee and keep thee. The Lord make His face shine upon thee, and be gracious unto thee. The

Lord lift up His countenance upon thee, and give thee peace."

I think these are about as sweet verses as we find in the Old Testament. I marked them years ago in my Bible, and many times I have turned over and read tnem. "The Lord lift up His countenance upon thee, and give thee peace." They remind us of the loving words of Jesus to his troubled disciples, "Peace, be still." The Jewish salutation used to be, as a man went into a house, "Peace be upon this house," and as he left the house the host would say, "Go in peace."

Then again, in the 14th chapter of John and the 27th verse, Jesus said : "Peace I leave with you, my peace I give unto you; not as the world giveth give I unto you. Let not your heart be troubled, neither let it be afraid." This is the precious legacy of Jesus to all His followers. Every man, every woman, every child, who believes in Him, may share in this portion. Christ has willed it to them, and His peace is theirs.

This then is our Lord's purpose and promise. My peace I give unto you. I give it, and I am not going to take it away again; I am going to leave it to you. "Not as the world giveth, give I unto you. Let not your heart be troubled, neither let it be afraid." But you know, when some men make their wills and deed away their property, there are some sharp, shrewd lawyers who will get hold of that will and break it all to pieces; they will go into court and break the will, and the jury will set the will aside, and the money goes into another channel. Now this will that Christ has made, neither devil nor man can break it. He has promised to give us peace, and there are thousands of witnesses who can say: "I have my part of that legacy. I have peace; I came to Him for peace, and I got it; I came to Him in darkness; I came to Him in trouble and sorrow; I was passing under a deep cloud of affliction, and I came to Him and He said, 'Peace, be still.' And from that hour peace reigned in my soul." Yes, many have proved the invitation true, "Come unto Me all ye that labor and are heavy laden, and I will give you rest." They found rest when they came. He is the author of rest, He is the author of peace, and no power can break that will; yea, unbelief may question it, but Jesus Christ rose to execute His own will, and it is in vain for man to contest it. Infidels and skeptics may tell us that it is all a myth, and that there isn't anything in it, and yet the glorious tidings is ever repeated, "Peace on earth, good will to man," and the poor and needy, the sad and sorrowful, are made partakers of it.

So, my reader, you need not wait for peace any longer. All you have to do is to enter into it to-day. You need not try to make peace. It is a false idea; you can not make it. Peace is already made by Jesus Christ, and is now declared unto you.

PEACE DECLARED.

When France and England were at war, a French vessel had gone off on a long voyage, a whaling voyage; and when they came back, the crew were short of water, and being now near an English port, they wanted to get water; but they were afraid that they would be taken if they went into that port; and some people in the port saw them, saw their signal of distress, and sent word to them that they need not be afraid, that the war was over, and peace had been declared. But they couldn't make those sailors believe it, and they didn't dare to go into port, although they were out of water; but at last they made up their minds that they had better go in and surrender up their cargo and surrender up their lives to their enemies than to perish at sea without water; but when they got in, they found out that peace had been declared, and that what had been told them was true. So there are a great many people who don't believe the glad tidings that peace has been made. Jesus Christ made peace on the Cross. He satisfied the claims of the law; and this law which condemns you and me has been fulfilled by Jesus Christ. He has made peace, and now He wants us just to enjoy it, just to believe it. Nor is there a thing to hinder us from doing it, if we will. We can enter into that blessing now, and have perfect peace. The promise is: "Thou wilt keep him in perfect peace whose mind is stayed on Thee. Trust ye in the Lord forever, for in the Lord Jehovah is everlasting strength." Now, as long as our mind is stayed on our dear selves, we will never have peace. Some people think more of themselves than of all the rest of the world. It is self in the morning, self at noon, and self at night. It is self when they wake up, and self when they go to bed; and they are all the time looking at themselves and thinking about themselves, instead of "looking unto Jesus." Faith is an outward look. Faith does not look within; it looks without. It is not what I think, nor what I feel, nor what I have done, but it is what Jesus Christ is and has done, and so we should trust in Him who is our strength, and whose strength will never fail. After Christ rose from the grave, three times, John tells us, He met His disciples and said unto them, "Peace be unto you." There is peace for the conscience through His blood, and peace for the heart in His love.

SECRET OF JOY.

Remember, then, that love is power, and peace is power; but now I will call attention to another fruit of the Spirit, and this too is power — the grace of JOY. It is the privilege, I believe, of every Christian to walk in the light, as God is in the light, and to have that peace which will be flowing unceasingly as we keep busy about His work. And it is our privilege to be full of the joy of the Lord. We read, that when Philip went down to Samaria and preached, there was great joy in the city. Why? Because they believed the glad tidings. And that is the natural order, joy in believing. When we believe the glad tidings, there comes a joy into our souls. Also we are told that our Lord sent the seventy out, and that they went forth preaching salvation in the name of Jesus Christ, and the result was that there were a great many who were blessed; and the seventy returned, it says, with great joy, and when they came back they said that the very devils were subject to them, through His name. The Lord seemed to just correct them in this one thing when He said, "Rejoice not that the devils are subject to you, but rejoice that your names are written in heaven." There is assurance for you. They had something to rejoice in now. God don't ask us to rejoice over nothing, but He gives us some ground for our joy. What would you think of a man or woman who seemed very happy to-day and full of joy, and couldn't tell you what made them so ? Suppose I should meet a man on the street, and he was so full of joy that he should get hold of both my hands and say, "Bless the Lord, I am so full of joy!" "What makes you so full of joy?" "Well, I don't know." "You don't know?" "No, I don't; but I am so joyful that I just want to get out of the flesh." "What makes you feel so joyful?" "Well, I don't know." Would we not think such a person unreasonable? But there are a great many people who feel—who want to feel—that they are Christians before they are Christians; they want the Christian's experience before they become Christians; they want to have the joy of the Lord before they receive Jesus Christ. But this is not the Gospel order. He brings joy when He comes, and we can not have joy apart from Him; there is no joy away from Him; He is the author of it, and we find our joy in Him.

JOY IS UNSELFISH.

Now, there are three kinds of joy; there is the joy of one's own salvation. I thought, when I first tasted that, it was the most delicious joy I had ever known, and that I could never get beyond it. But I found, afterward, there was something more joyful than that, namely, the joy of the salvation of others. Oh, the privilege, the blessed privilege, to be used of God to win a soul to Christ, and to see a man or woman being led out of bondage by some act of ours toward them. To think that God should condescend to allow us to be co-workers with Him. It is the highest honor we can wear. It surpasses the joy of our own salvation, this joy of seeing others saved. And then John said, He had no greater joy than to see His disciples walking in the truth. Every man who has been the means of leading souls to Christ understands what that means. Young disciples, walk in the truth and you will have joy all the while.

I think there is a difference between happiness and joy. Happiness is caused by things which happen around me, and circumstances will mar it, but joy flows right on through trouble; joy flows on through the dark; joy flows in the night as well as in the day; joy flows all through persecution and opposition; it flows right along, for it is an unceasing fountain bubbling up in the heart; a secret spring which the world can't see and don't know anything about; but the Lord gives His people perpetual joy when they walk in obedience to Him.

This joy is fed by the Divine Word. Jeremiah says in chapter xv, 16: "Thy words were found, and I did eat them; and Thy Word was unto me the joy and rejoicing of my heart; for I am called by Thy name, O Lord."

He ate the words, and what was the result? He said they were the joy and rejoicing of his heart. Now people should look for joy in the Word, and not in the world; they should look for the joy which the Scriptures furnish, and then go work in the vineyard; because a joy that don't send me out to some one else, a joy that don't impel me to go and help the poor drunkard, a joy that don't prompt me to visit the widow and the fatherless, a joy that don't cause me to go into the Mission Sunday-school or other Christian work, is not worth having, and is not from above; a joy that does not constrain me to go and work for the **Master**, is purely sentiment and not real joy.

JOY IN PERSECUTION.

Then it says in Luke vi, 22 : " Blessed are ye when men shall hate you, and when they shall separate you from their company, and shall reproach you and cast out your name as evil, for the Son of Man's sake. Rejoice ye in that day and leap for joy, for behold your reward is great in heaven ; for in like manner did their fathers unto the prophets."

Christians do not receive their reward down here. We have to go right against the current of the world. We may be unpopular, and we may go right against many of our personal friends if we live godly in Christ Jesus; and at the same time, if we are persecuted for the Master's sake, we will have this joy bubbling up; it just comes right up in our hearts all the while—a joy that is unceasing—that flows right on. The world can not choke that fountain. If we have Christ in the heart, by and by the reward will come. The longer I live the more I am convinced that godly men and women are not appreciated in our day. But their work will live after them, and there will be a greater work done after they are gone, by the influence of their lives, than when they were living. Daniel is doing a thousand times more than when he was living in Babylon. Abraham is doing more to-day than he did on the plain with his tent and altar. All these centuries he has been living, and so we read, " Blessed are the dead that die in the Lord, from henceforth ; yea saith the Spirit, that they may rest from their labors, and their works do follow them."

Let us set the streams running that shall flow on after we have gone. If we have to-day persecution and opposition, let us press forward, and our reward will be great by and by. Oh! think of this; the Lord Jesus, the Maker of heaven and earth, who created the world, says, "Great shall be thy reward." He calls it great. If some friend should say it is great, it might be very small; but when the Lord, the great and mighty God, says it is great, what must it be? Oh! the reward that is in store for those who serve Him! We have this joy, if we serve Him. A man or woman is not fit to work for God who is cast down, because they go about their work with a tell-tale face. "The joy of the Lord is your strength." What we need to-day is a joyful church. A joyful church will make inroads upon the works of Satan, and we will see the Gospel going down into dark lanes and dark alleys, and into dark garrets and cellars, and we will see the drunkards reached and the gamblers and the harlots come pressing into the kingdom of God. It is this carrying a sad countenance, with so many wrinkles on our brows, that retards Christianity. Oh may there come great joy upon believers everywhere, that we may shout for joy and rejoice in God day and night. A joyful church—let us pray for that, that the Lord may make us joyful, and when we have joy, then we will have success; and if we don't have the reward we think we should have here, let us constantly remember the rewarding time will come hereafter.

Some one has said, if you had asked men in Abraham's day who their great man was, they would have said Enoch, and not Abraham. If you had asked in Moses' day who their great man was, they would not have said it was Moses; he was nothing, but it would have been Abraham. If you had asked in the days of Elijah or Daniel, it wouldn't have been Daniel or Elijah; they were nothing; but it would have been Moses. And in the days of Jesus Christ—if you had asked in the days of Jesus Christ about John the Baptist or the apostles, you would hear they were mean and contemptible in the sight of the world, and were looked upon with scorn and reproach; but see how mighty they have become. And so we will not be appreciated in our day, but we are to toil on and work on, possessing this joy all the while. And if we lack it, let us cry: "Restore unto me the joy of Thy salvation, and uphold me with Thy free Spirit; then will I teach transgressors Thy ways, and sinners shall be converted unto Thee."

Again, the 15th chapter of John, and 11th verse, reads: "These things have I spoken unto you, that my joy might remain in you, and that your joy might be full." And in the 16th chapter and 22d verse: "And ye now therefore have sorrow; but I will see you again, and your heart shall rejoice, and your joy no man taketh from you."

I am so thankful that I have a joy that the world can not rob me of; I have a treasure that the world can not take from me; I have something that it is not in the power of man or devil to deprive me of, and that is the joy of the Lord. "No man taketh it from you." In the second century, they brought a martyr before a king, and the king wanted him to recant and give up Christ and Christianity, but the man spurned the proposition. But the king said: "If you don't do it, I will banish you." The man smiled and answered: "You can't banish me from Christ, for He says He will never leave me nor forsake me." The king got angry, and said: "Well, I will confiscate your property and take it all from you." And the man replied: "My treasures are laid up on high; you can not get them." The king became still more angry, and said: "I will kill you." "Why," the man answered, "I have been dead forty years; I have been dead with Christ; dead to the world, and my life is hid with Christ in God, and you can not touch it." And so we can rejoice, because we are on resurrection ground, having risen with Christ. Let persecution and opposition come, we can rejoice continually, and remember that our reward is great, reserved for us unto the day when He who is our Life shall appear, and we shall appear with Him in glory.

"THE Spirit, oh, sinner,
    In mercy doth move
  Thy heart, so long hardened,
    Of sin to reprove;
Resist not the Spirit,
    Nor longer delay;
God's gracious entreaties may end with to-day.

  "Oh, child of the kingdom,
    From sin service cease;
  Be filled with the Spirit,
    With comfort and peace.
  Oh, *grieve* not the Spirit,
    Thy Teacher is He,
That Jesus, thy Saviour, may glorified be.

  "Defiled is the temple,
    Its beauty laid low,
  On God's holy altar
    The embers faint glow,
  By love yet rekindled,
    A flame may be fanned;
Oh, *quench* not the Spirit, *the Lord is at hand!* "

—P. P. Bliss.

CHAPTER V.

POWER HINDERED.

The strokes of the "Sword of the Spirit" alight only on the conscience, and its edge is anointed with a balm to heal every wound it may inflict.—*Dr. J. Harris*.

Every vain thought and idle word, and every wicked deed, is like so many drops to quench the Spirit of God. Some quench Him with the lust of the flesh; some quench Him with cares of the mind; some quench Him with long delays, that is, not plying the motion when it cometh, but crossing the good thoughts with bad thoughts, and doing a thing when the Spirit saith not. The Spirit is often grieved before He be quenched.—*H. Smith.*

In times when vile men held the high places of the land, a roll of drums was employed to drown the martyr's voice, lest the testimony of truth from the scaffold should reach the ears of the people,—an illustration of how men deal with their own consciences, and seek to put to silence the truth-telling voice of the Holy Spirit.—*Arnot.*

POWER HINDERED.

Israel, we are told, limited the Holy One of Israel. They vexed and grieved the Holy Spirit, and rebelled against His authority, but there is a special sin against Him, which we may profitably consider. The first description of it is in Matthew xii, 22d verse:

THE UNPARDONABLE SIN.

"Then was brought unto Him one possessed with a devil, blind and dumb; and He healed him, insomuch that the blind and dumb both spake and saw. And all the people were amazed, and said, Is not this the son of David? But when the Pharisees heard it, they said, This fellow doth not cast out devils, but by Beelzebub the prince of the devils. And Jesus knew their thoughts, and said unto them, Every kingdom divided against itself is brought to desolation; and every city or house divided against itself shall not stand. And if Satan cast out Satan, he is divided against himself; how shall then his kingdom stand? And if I by Beelzebub cast out devils, by whom do your children cast them out? therefore they shall be your judges. But if I cast out devils by the Spirit of God, then the kingdom of God is come unto you. Or else how can one enter into a strong man's house, and spoil his goods, except he first bind the strong man? and then he will spoil his house. He that is not with me is against me; and he that gathereth not with me, scattereth abroad. Wherefore I say unto you, all manner of sin and blasphemy shall be forgiven unto men; but the blasphemy against the Holy Ghost shall not be forgiven unto men. And whosoever speaketh a word against the Son of man, it shall be forgiven him; but whosoever speaketh against the Holy Ghost, it shall not be forgiven him, neither in this world, neither in the world to come." That is Matthew's account. Now let us read Mark's account in chapter iii, 21, etc.:

"And when His friends heard of it, they went out to lay hold on Him, for they said: He (that is Christ) is beside Himself. And the scribes which came down from Jerusalem said, He hath Beelzebub, and by the prince of the devils casteth He out devils."

The word Beelzebub means the Lord of Filth. They charged the Lord Jesus with being possessed not only with an evil spirit, but with a filthy spirit.

"And He called them unto Him, and said unto them in parables, How can Satan cast out Satan? And if a kingdom be divided against itself, that kingdom can not stand. And if a house be divided against itself, that house can not stand. And if Satan rise up against himself, and be divided, he can not stand, but hath an end. No man can enter into a strong man's house, and spoil his goods, except he will first bind the strong man; and then he will spoil his house. Verily I say unto you, all sins shall be forgiven unto the sons of men, and blasphemies wherewith soever they shall blaspheme: But he that shall blaspheme against the Holy Ghost hath never forgiveness, but is in danger of eternal damnation."

Now, if it stopped there, we would be left perhaps in darkness, and we would not exactly understand what the sin against the Holy Ghost is; but the next verse of this same chapter of Mark just throws light upon the whole matter, and we need not be in darkness another minute if we really want light; for observe, the verse reads: "Because they said, He hath an unclean spirit."

Now, I have met a good many atheists and skeptics and deists and infidels, both in this country and abroad, but I never in my life met a man or woman who ever said that Jesus Christ was possessed of an unclean devil. Did you? I don't think you ever met such a person. I have heard men say bitter things against Christ, but I never heard any man stand up and say that he thought Jesus Christ was possessed with the devil, and that he cast out devils by the power of the devil; and I don't believe any man or woman has any right to say they have committed the unpardonable sin, unless they have maliciously, and wilfully and deliberately said that they believe that Jesus Christ had a devil in Him, and that He was under the power of the devil, and that He cast out devils by the power of the devil. Because you perhaps have heard some one say that there is such a thing as grieving the Spirit of God, and resisting the Spirit of God until He has taken His flight and left you, then you have said "That is the unpardonable sin."

WHAT IT IS NOT.

I admit there is such a thing as resisting the Spirit of God, and resisting till the Spirit of God has departed; but if the Spirit of God has left any, they will not be troubled about their sins. The very fact that they are troubled, shows that the Spirit of God has not left them. If a man is troubled about his sins, it is the work of the Spirit; for Satan never yet told him he was a sinner. Satan makes us believe that we are pretty good; that we are good enough without God, safe without Christ, and that we don't need salvation. But when a man wakes up to the fact that he is lost, that he is a sinner, that is the work of the Spirit; and if the Spirit of God had left him, he would not be in that state; and just because men and women want to be Christians, is a sign that the Spirit of God is drawing them.

If resisting the Spirit of God is an unpardonable sin, then we have all committed it, and there is no hope for any of us; for I do not believe there is a minister, or a worker in Christ's vineyard, who has not, some time in his life, resisted the Holy Ghost; who has not some time in his life rejected the Spirit of God. To resist the Holy Ghost is one thing, and to commit that awful sin of blasphemy against the Holy Ghost, is another thing; and we want to take the Scripture and just compare them. Now, some people say, "I have such blasphemous thoughts; there are some awful thoughts that come into my mind against God," and they think that is the unpardonable sin. We are not to blame for having

BAD THOUGHTS

come into our minds. If we harbor them, then we are to blame. But if the devil comes and darts an evil thought into my mind, and I say, "Lord help me," sin is not reckoned to me. Who has not had evil thoughts come into his mind, flash into his heart, and been called to fight them!

One old divine says, "You are not to blame for the birds that fly over your head, but if you allow them to come down and make a nest in your hair, then you are to blame. You are to blame if you don't fight them off." And so with these evil thoughts that come flashing into our minds; we have to fight them, we are not to harbor them; we are not to entertain them. If I have evil thoughts come into my mind, and evil desires, it is no sign that I have committed the unpardonable sin. If I love these thoughts and harbor them, and think evil of God, and think Jesus Christ a blasphemer, I am responsible for such gross iniquity ; but if I charge Him with being the prince of devils, then I am committing the unpardonable sin.

THE FAITHFUL FRIEND.

Let us now consider the sin of "Grieving the Spirit." *Resisting* the Holy Ghost is one thing, *grieving* Him is another. Stephen charged the unbelieving Jews in the 7th chapter of Acts, "Ye do always resist the Holy Ghost as your fathers did, so do ye." The world has always been resisting the Spirit of God in all ages. That is the history of the world. The world is to-day resisting the Holy Spirit.

"Faithful are the wounds of a friend." The Divine Spirit as a friend reveals to this poor world its faults, and the world only hates Him for it. He shows them the plague of their hearts. He convinces or convicts them of sin, therefore they fight the Spirit of God. I believe there is many a man resisting the Holy Ghost; I believe there is many a man to-day fighting against the Spirit of God.

In the 4th chapter of Ephesians, in the 30th, 31st, and 32d verses, we read:

"And grieve not the Holy Spirit of God, whereby ye are sealed unto the day of redemption. Let all bitterness, and wrath, and anger, and clamor, and evil speaking be put away from you, with all malice. And be ye kind, one to another, tender-hearted, forgiving one another, even as God for Christ's sake hath forgiven you."

Now, mark you, that was written to the Church at Ephesus. "Grieve not the Holy Spirit, whereby ye are sealed unto the day of redemption." I believe to-day the Church all over Christendom is guilty of grieving the Holy Spirit. There are a good many believers in different churches wondering why the work of God is not revived.

THE CHURCH GRIEVES THE SPIRIT.

I think that if we search, we will find something in the Church grieving the Spirit of God; it may be a mere schism in the church; it may be some unsound doctrine; it may be some division in the Church. There is one thing I have noticed as I have traveled in different countries; I never yet have known the Spirit of God to work where the Lord's people were divided. There is one thing that we must have if we are to have the Holy Spirit of God to work in our midst, and that is unity. If a church is divided, the members should immediately seek unity. Let the believers come together and get the difficulty out of the way. If the minister of a church can not unite the people, if those that were dissatisfied will not fall in, it would be better for that minister to retire. I think there are a good many ministers in this country who are losing their time; they have lost, some of them, months and years; they have not seen any fruit, and they will not see any fruit, because they have a divided church. Such a church can not grow in divine things. The Spirit of God don't work where there is division, and what we want to-day is the spirit of unity amongst God's children, so that the Lord may work.

WORLDLY AMUSEMENTS.

Then, another thing, I think, that grieves the Spirit, is the miserable policy of introducing questionable entertainments. There are the lotteries, for instance, that we have in many churches. If a man wants to gamble, he doesn't have to go to some gambling den; he can stay in the church. And there are fairs—bazaars, as they call them—where they have rafflings and grab-bags. And if he wants to see a drama, he don't need to go to the theater, for many of our churches are turned into theaters; he may stay right in the church and witness the acting. I believe all these things grieve the Spirit of God. I believe when we bring the Church down to the level of the world to reach the world, we are losing all the while and grieving the Spirit of God.

But some say, if we take that standard and lift it up high, it will drive away a great many members from our churches. I believe it, and I think the quicker they are gone the better. The world has come into the Church like a flood, and how often you find an ungodly choir employed to do the singing for the whole congretion; the idea that we need an ungodly man to sing praises to God! It was not long ago I heard of a church where they had an unconverted choir, and the minister saw something about the choir that he didn't like, and he spoke to the chorister, but the chorister replied: "You attend to your end of the church, and I will attend to mine." You can not expect the Spirit of God to work in a church in such a state as that.

UNCONVERTED CHOIRS.

Paul tells us not to speak in an unknown tongue, and if we have choirs who are singing in an unknown tongue, why is not that just as great an abomination? I have been in churches where they have had a choir, who would rise and sing, and sing, and it seemed as if they sung five or ten minutes, and I could not understand one solitary word they sung, and all the while the people were looking around carelessly. There are, perhaps, a select few, very fond of fine music, and they want to bring the opera right into the church, and so they have opera music in the church, and the people, who are drowsy and sleepy, don't take part in the singing. They hire ungodly men, unconverted men, and these men will sometimes get the Sunday paper, and get back in the organ loft, and the moment the minister begins his sermon, they will take out their papers and read them all the while that the minister is preaching. The organist, provided he does not go out for a walk—if he happens to keep awake, will read his paper, or, perhaps, a novel, while the minister is preaching; and the minister wonders why God don't revive His work; he wonders why he is losing his hold on the congregation; he wonders why people don't come crowding into the church; why people are running after the world instead of coming into the church. The trouble is that we have let down the standard; we have grieved the Spirit of God. One movement of God's power is worth more than all our artificial power, and what the Church of God wants to-day is to get down in the dust of humiliation and confession of sin, and go out and be separated from the world; and then see if we do not have power with God and with man.

WHAT IS SUCCESS?

The Gospel has not lost its power; it is just as powerful to-day as it ever has been. We don't wan't any new doctrine. It is still the old Gospel with the old power, the Holy Ghost power; and if the churches will but confess their sins and put them away, and lift the standard instead of pulling it down, and pray to God to lift us all up into a higher and holier life, then the fear of the Lord will come upon the people around us.

It was when Jacob put away strange gods and set his face toward Bethel that the fear of God fell upon the nations around. And when the churches turn towards God, and we cease grieving the Spirit, so that He may work through us, we will then have conversions all the while. Believers will be added to the Church daily. It is sad when you look over Christendom and see how desolate it is, and see how little spiritual life, spiritual power, there is in the Church of God to-day, many of the church members not even wanting this Holy Ghost power. They don't desire it; they want intellectual power; they want to get some man who will just draw; and a choir that will draw; not caring whether any one is saved. With them that is not the question. Only fill the pews, have good society, fashionable people, and dancing; such persons are found one night at the theater and the next night at the opera. They don't like the prayer-meetings; they abominate them; if the minister will only lecture and entertain, that would suit them. I said to a man some time ago, "How are you getting on at your church?" "Oh, splendid." "Many conversions?" "Well—well, on that side we are not getting on so well. But," he said, "we rented all our pews and are able to pay all our running expenses; we are getting on splendidly." That is what the godless call "getting on splendidly;" because they rent the pews, pay the minister, and pay all the running expenses. Conversions! that is a strange thing. There was a man being shown through one of the cathedrals of Europe; he had come in from the country, and one of the men belonging to the cathedral was showing him around, when he inquired, "Do you have many conversions here?" "Many what?" "Many conversions here?" "Ah, man, this is not a Wesleyan chapel." The idea of there being conversions there! And you can go into a good many churches in this country and ask if they have many conversions there, and they would not know what it meant, they are so far away from the Lord; they are not looking for conversions, and don't expect them.

SHIPWRECKS.

Alas! how many young converts have made shipwreck against such churches. Instead of being a harbor of delight to them, they have proved false lights, alluring them to destruction. Isn't it time for us to get down on our faces before God and cry mightily to Him to forgive us our sins. The quicker we own it the better. You may be invited to a party, and it may be made up of church members, and what will be the conversation? Oh, I got so sick of such parties that I left years ago; I would not think of spending a night that way; it is a waste of time; there is hardly a chance to say a word for the Master. If you talk of a personal Christ, your company becomes offensive; they don't like it; they want you to talk about the world, about a popular minister, a popular church, a good organ, a good choir, and they say, "Oh, we have a grand organ, and a superb choir," and all that, and it suits them; but that don't warm the Christian heart. When you speak of a risen Christ and a personal Saviour, they don't like it; the fact is, the world has come into the church and taken possession of it, and what we want to do is to wake up and ask God to forgive us for "Grieving the Spirit."

Dear reader, search your heart and inquire, Have I done anything to grieve the Spirit of God? If you have, may God show it to you to-day; if you have done any thing to grieve the Spirit of God, you want to know it to-day, and get down on your face before God and ask Him to forgive you and help you to put it away. I have lived long enough to know that if I can not have the power of the Spirit of God on me to help me to work for Him, I would rather die, than live just for the sake of living. How many are there in the church to-day, who have been members for fifteen or twenty years, but have never done a solitary thing for Jesus

Christ? They can not lay their hands upon one solitary soul who has been blessed through their influence; they can not point to-day to one single person who has ever been lifted up by them.

QUENCH NOT.

In 1st Thessalonians, 5th chapter, we are told not to Quench the Spirit. Now, I am confident the cares of the world are coming in and quenching the Spirit with a great many. They say: "I don't care for the world;" perhaps not the *pleasures* of the world so much after all as the *cares* of this life; but they have just let the cares come in and quench the Spirit of God. Anything that comes between me and God—between my soul and God—quenches the Spirit. It may be my family. You may say: "Is there any danger of my loving my family too much?" Not if we love God more; but God must have the first place. If I love my family more than God, then I am quenching the Spirit of God within me; if I love wealth, if I love fame, if I love honor, if I love position, if I love pleasure, if I love self, more than I love God who created and saved me, then I am committing a sin; I am not only grieving the Spirit of God, but quenching Him, and robbing my soul of His power.

EMBLEMS OF THE SPIRIT.

But I would further call attention to the emblems of the Holy Spirit. An emblem is something that represents an object; the same as a balance is an emblem of justice, and a crown an emblem of royalty, and a scepter is an emblem of power; so we find in the 17th chapter of Exodus and 6th verse, that water is an emblem of the Holy Spirit. You find in the Smitten Rock, in the wilderness, the work of the Trinity illustrated.

"Behold, I will stand before thee there upon the rock in Horeb; and thou shall smite the rock, and there shall come water out of it, that the people may drink. And Moses did so, in the sight of the elders of Israel."

Paul declares, in Corinthians, that the rock was Christ; it represented Christ. God says: "I will stand upon the rock," and as Moses smote the rock the water came out, which was an emblem of the Holy Spirit; and it flowed out along through the camp; and they drank of the water. Now water is cleansing; it is fertilizing; it is refreshing; it is abundant, and it is freely given; and so the Spirit of God is the same: cleansing, fertilizing, refreshing, reviving, and He was freely given when the smitten Christ was glorified. Then, too, fire is an emblem of the Spirit; it is purifying, illuminating, searching. We talk about searching our hearts. We can not do it. What we want is to have God search them. O that God may search us and bring out the hidden things, the secret things that cluster there and bring them to light. The wind is another emblem. It is independent, powerful, sensible in its effects, and reviving; how the Spirit of God revives when He comes to all the drooping members of the Church. Then the rain and the dew—fertilizing, refreshing, abundant; and the dove, gentle—what more gentle than the dove; and the lamb?—gentle, meek, innocent, a sacrifice. We read of the wrath of God; we read of the wrath of the Lamb, but nowhere do we read of the wrath of the Holy Spirit—gentle, innocent, meek, loving; and that Spirit wants to take possession of our hearts. And He comes as a voice, another emblem—speaking, guiding, warning, teaching; and the seal—impressing, securing, and making us as His own. May we know Him in all His wealth of blessing. This is my prayer for myself—for you. May we heed the words of the grand Apostle: "My speech and my preaching was not with enticing words of man's wisdom, but in demonstration of the Spirit, and of power: that your faith should not stand IN THE WISDOM OF MEN, BUT IN THE POWER OF GOD."

By Dwight L. Moody

"These are popular works by our great Evangelist; and they deserve a large sale. There can be no need for us to commend the living, blazing speech of our brother Moody. Who can equal him in natural simplicity all aglow with holy passion?"
—C. H. SPURGEON.

Notes From My Bible; from Genesis to Revelation............................$1.00
Sowing and Reaping. 12mo............ .50
Pleasure and Profit in Bible Study. *92d thousand.*

Sovereign Grace. *48th thousand.*
Bible Characters. *27th thousand.*
Prevailing Prayer—What Hinders It? *70th thousand.*
To the Work! To the Work! *60th thousand.*
The Way to God and How to Find It. *425th thousand.*
Heaven. *170th thousand.*
Secret Power. *106th thousand.*
Twelve Select Sermons. *225th thousand.*
The D. L. Moody Library, comprising the eight last named books. Each, paper.... .25
   cloth... .50
   Bound in four volumes, 12mo, cloth, boxed, 4.00
The Full Assurance of Faith. Paper... .10
   flexible cloth..................................... .20
How to Study the Bible. Revised. *80th thousand.* Paper, 10c.; flexible cloth...... .15
The Way and the Word. *112th thousand.* Paper, 10c ; cloth........................... .20
The Second Coming of Christ. *65th thousand.* Paper.................................. .10
Gospel Booklets. Per dozen, 35c.; per hundred, net................................. 2.50
Inquiry Meetings. By Moody and Whittle. 16mo, paper.............................. .10
D. L. Moody at Home. 12mo, paper.. .50
   cloth.. 1.00
Moody in Chicago. World's Fair campaign, by Rev. E. B. Hartzler. 12mo, cloth.. 1.00

By Rev. A. J. Gordon, D.D.

Adoniram Judson Gordon. A Biography. By his son, Ernest B Gordon. With portraits and other illustrations 8vo, cloth.................................$1.50

The Ministry of the Spirit. Introduction by Rev. F. B. Meyer. B.A. 12mo, cloth, gilt top............ 1.00
CHEAP EDITION, 18mo, cloth, net, 25c.; by post, net, .30

How Christ Came to Church: The Pastor's Dream. A Spiritual Autobiography. With the life-story and the dream as interpreting the man, by Rev. A. T. Pierson, D.D. With portrait. 8vo, cloth, gilt top.... .75
CHEAP EDITION, 18mo, cloth, net, 25c.; by post, net, .30

In Christ; or, The Believer's Union with his Lord. 12mo, cloth, gilt top, $1.00; paper..............net .35
POCKET EDITION, Long 18mo cloth............ 1 00
CHEAP EDITION, 18mo, cloth, net, 25c.; by post, net, .30

The Holy Spirit in Missions. 12mo, cloth, gilt top. 1.25

Grace and Glory. Sermons for the Life that Now is and That which is to Come. 12mo, cloth, gilt top, 1.50. Paper..............................net, .50

Ecce Venit; or, Behold He Cometh. 12mo, cloth, gilt top, $1.25; paper......................net, .50

The Ministry of Healing; or, Miracles of Cures in all ages. With History of the Doctrine from the Earliest Times. 12mo, cloth, gilt top, $1.25; paper, net, .50

The Two-fold Life; or, Christ's Work for Us, and Christ's Work in Us. 12mo, cloth, gilt top..... 1.25
Paper..net, .50

Risen with Christ; or, The Resurrection of Christ and of the Believer. 16mo. boards............... .30

The First Thing in the World; or, The Primacy of Faith. 16mo, Popular Vellum Series.......... .20
CHEAP EDITION, net, 10c.; per doz...........net, 1.00

The Coronation Hymnal. 400 Hymns, with Music. By Rev. Drs. A. J. Gordon and A. T. Pierson. 4to, half-cloth, red edges, net, 60c.; cloth, red edges, net .75
Two editions: An edition for general use, and a Baptist edition. Send for specimen pages.

Fleming H. Revell Company

NEW YORK: 112 Fifth Ave.
CHICAGO: 63 Washington St.
TORONTO: 140 & 142 Yonge St.

RECEIVED YE THE HOLY GHOST?

Received
Ye The
Holy
Ghost?

By J. WILBUR CHAPMAN, D.D.
AUTHOR OF
"THE IVORY PALACES OF THE KING," ETC.

FLEMING H. REVELL COMPANY
NEW YORK   PUBLISHERS
CHICAGO   OF EVANGELICAL
TORONTO   LITERATURE

Copyright
1894
FLEMING H. REVELL COMPANY

TO

Mr. D. L. Moody

AND TO

Rev. F. B. Meyer

THIS BOOK IS GRATEFULLY DEDICATED

To the former, because in his public ministry and private life he has been a great inspiration. To the latter, because two years ago, in a single sentence, he opened up a new life to me when he led me to know more about the Spirit of God.

Under God, to both of these, his servants, I owe an inexpressible debt of gratitude.

CONTENTS

CAP	PAGE
1. What saith the Scripture?	9
2. How may I Know Him?	31
3. How may I Receive Him?	65
4. What of the Result?	101

RECEIVED YE THE HOLY GHOST?

WHAT SAITH THE SCRIPTURE?

Cap I

WHAT SAITH THE SCRIPTURE?

"Search the Scriptures; for in them ye think ye have eternal life: and they are they which testify of me."—John v. 39.

ATTRIBUTES OF THE HOLY SPIRIT.—Gen. i. 2: And the Spirit of God moved upon the face of the waters. Job xxxiii. 4: The Spirit of God hath made me, and the breath of the Almighty hath given me life. Ps. cxxxix. 7: Whither shall I go from thy Spirit? or whither shall I flee from thy presence? Isa. xl. 13: Who hath directed the Spirit of the Lord, or being his counselor hath taught him? Zech. iv. 6: Not by might, nor by power, but by my Spirit, saith the Lord of hosts. Luke i. 35: The Holy Ghost shall come upon thee, and the power of the Highest shall overshadow thee: therefore also that holy thing which shall be born of thee shall be called the Son of God. John vi. 63: It is the Spirit that quickeneth. Acts v. 3: Why hath Satan filled thine heart to lie to the Holy Ghost? 4: Thou hast not lied unto men, but unto God. 1 Cor. ii. 10: But God hath revealed them unto us by his Spirit: for the Spirit searcheth all things, yea, the deep things of God. 11: For what man knoweth the things of a man, save the spirit of man which is in him? even so the things of God knoweth no man, but the Spirit of God. Heb. ix. 14: The eternal Spirit. Heb. x. 29: The Spirit of grace. 1 Peter iv. 14: The Spirit of glory and of God resteth upon you. Rev. iv. 5: Seven lamps of fire burning before the throne, which are the seven Spirits of God. Rev. xi. 11: The Spirit of life from God.

MIRACULOUS INFLUENCES OF THE HOLY SPIRIT.—Joel ii. 28, 29: And it shall come to pass afterward, that I will pour out my Spirit upon all flesh; and your sons and your daughters shall prophesy, your old men shall dream dreams, your young men shall see visions: and also upon the servants and upon the handmaids in those days will I pour out my Spirit. Matt. xii. 28: But if I cast out devils by the Spirit of God, then the kingdom of

RECEIVED YE THE HOLY GHOST?

God is come unto you. Acts i. 5, 8: For John truly baptized with water; but ye shall be baptized with the Holy Ghost not many days hence. But ye shall receive power, after that the Holy Ghost is come upon you: and ye shall be witnesses unto me both in Jerusalem, and in all Judea, and in Samaria, and unto the uttermost part of the earth. Acts ii. 2–4: And suddenly there came a sound from heaven as of a rushing mighty wind, and it filled all the house where they were sitting. And there appeared unto them cloven tongues like as of fire, and it sat upon each of them. And they were all filled with the Holy Ghost, and began to speak with other tongues, as the Spirit gave them utterance. Acts viii. 15–17: Who, when they were come down, prayed for them, that they might receive the Holy Ghost: (for as yet he was fallen upon none of them: only they were baptized in the name of the Lord Jesus.) Then laid they their hands on them, and they received the Holy Ghost. Acts x. 44, 46: While Peter yet spake these words, the Holy Ghost fell on all them which heard the word. For they heard them speak with tongues, and magnify God. Acts xix. 2–6: He said unto them, Have ye received the Holy Ghost since ye believed? And they said unto him, We have not so much as heard whether there be any Holy Ghost. And he said unto them, Unto what then were ye baptized? And they said, Unto John's baptism. Then said Paul, John verily baptized with the baptism of repentance, saying unto the people, that they should believe on him which should come after him, that is, on Christ Jesus. When they heard this, they were baptized in the name of the Lord Jesus. And when Paul had laid his hands upon them, the Holy Ghost came on them; and they spake with tongues, and prophesied. 1 Cor. xii. 9–11: To another faith by the same Spirit; to another the gifts of healing by the same Spirit; to another the working of miracles; to another prophecy; to another discerning of spirits; to another divers kinds of tongues; to another the interpretation of tongues: but all these worketh that one and the selfsame Spirit, dividing to every man severally as he will. Gal. iii. 5: He therefore that ministereth to you the Spirit, and worketh miracles among you, doeth he it by the works of the law, or by the hearing of faith? Heb. ii. 4: God also bearing them witness, both with signs and wonders, and with divers miracles, and gifts of the Holy Ghost, according to his own will.

PRAYER FOR THE HOLY SPIRIT.—
Ps. li. 11: Take not thy Holy Spirit from me. 12: Uphold me with thy free Spirit. Luke xi. 13: If ye then, being evil, know how to give good gifts unto your children: how much more shall your heavenly Father give the Holy Spirit to them that ask him? Acts iv. 31: When they had prayed, the place was shaken where they were assembled together; and they were all filled with the Holy Ghost. Eph. iii. 16: That he would grant you, according to the riches of his glory, to be strengthened with might by his Spirit in the inner man.

RECEIVED YE THE HOLY GHOST?

SINS AGAINST THE HOLY SPIRIT.—
Isa. lxiii. 10: They rebelled, and vexed his Holy Spirit: therefore he was turned to be their enemy. Matt. xii. 31: But the blasphemy against the Holy Ghost shall not be forgiven unto men. 32: And whosoever speaketh a word against the Son of man, it shall be forgiven him: but whosoever speaketh against the Holy Ghost, it shall not be forgiven him, neither in this world, neither in the world to come. Mark iii. 29: But he that shall blaspheme against the Holy Ghost hath never forgiveness, but is in danger of eternal damnation. Acts vii. 51: Ye do always resist the Holy Ghost: as your fathers did, so do ye. Acts viii. 18–20: And when Simon saw that through laying on of the Apostles' hands the Holy Ghost was

given, he offered them money, saying, Give me also this power, that on whomsoever I lay hands, he may receive the Holy Ghost. But Peter said unto him, Thy money perish with thee, because thou hast thought that the gift of God may be purchased with money. **Eph. iv. 30:** Grieve not the Holy Spirit of God. **1 Thess. v. 19:** Quench not the Spirit. **Heb. x. 29:** Of how much sorer punishment, suppose ye, shall he be thought worthy, who hath . . . done despite unto the Spirit of grace? **Rev. ii. 7:** He that hath an ear, let him hear what the Spirit saith unto the churches.

THE WORK AND INFLUENCE OF THE HOLY SPIRIT.—**Gen. vi. 3:** My Spirit shall not always strive with man. **Isa. xliv. 3:** For I will pour water upon him that is thirsty, and floods upon the dry ground: I will pour my Spirit upon thy seed, and my blessing upon thine offspring. 4: And they shall spring up as among the grass, as willows by the watercourses. Isa. lix. 19: When the enemy shall come in like a flood, the Spirit of the Lord shall lift up a standard against him. 21: My Spirit that is upon thee, and my words which I have put in thy mouth, shall not depart out of thy mouth, nor out of the mouth of thy seed. Ezek. xxxix. 29: Neither will I hide my face any more from them: for I have poured out my Spirit upon the house of Israel. Hag. ii. 5: According to the word that I covenanted with you when ye came out of Egypt, so my Spirit remaineth among you. Zech. xii. 10: I will pour upon the house of David, and upon the inhabitants of Jerusalem, the spirit of grace and of supplications: and they shall look upon me whom they have pierced, and they shall mourn. Matt. iii. 11: I indeed baptize you with water unto repentance: but . . . he shall baptize you with the Holy Ghost, and with fire. John iv. 14: Whosoever drinketh of the water that I shall give him shall never thirst; but the water that I shall give him shall be in him a well of water springing up into everlasting life. John vii. 38: He that believeth on me, as the Scripture hath said, out of his belly shall flow rivers of living water. 39: (But this spake he of the Spirit, which they that believe on him should receive: for the Holy Ghost was not yet given; because that Jesus was not yet glorified.) John xiv. 16, 17: I will pray the

Father, and he shall give you another Comforter, that he may abide with you forever; even the Spirit of truth; whom the world cannot receive, because it seeth him not, neither knoweth him: but ye know him; for he dwelleth with you, and shall be in you. John xv. 26: When the Comforter is come, whom I will send unto you from the Father, even the Spirit of truth, which proceedeth from the Father, he shall testify of me. John xvi. 7: It is expedient for you that I go away: for if I go not away, the Comforter will not come unto you; but if I depart, I will send him unto you. 8: When he is come, he will reprove the world of sin, and of righteousness, and of judgment. John xx. 22: He breathed on them, and saith unto them, Receive ye the Holy Ghost. Acts

ii. 38: Repent, and be baptized every one of you in the name of Jesus Christ for the remission of sins, and ye shall receive the gift of the Holy Ghost. Acts iii. 19: That your sins may be blotted out, when the times of refreshing shall come from the presence of the Lord. Acts v. 32: We are his witnesses of these things; and so is also the Holy Ghost, whom God hath given to them that obey him: Acts vi. 5: They chose Stephen, a man full of faith and of the Holy Ghost. Acts ix. 31: Walking in the fear of the Lord, and in the comfort of the Holy Ghost, were multiplied. Acts x. 44: The Holy Ghost fell on all them which heard the word. 45: And they of the circumcision which believed were astonished, as many as came with Peter, because that on the Gentiles also

RECEIVED YE THE HOLY GHOST?

was poured out the gift of the Holy Ghost. Acts xi. 24: He was a good man, and full of the Holy Ghost. Acts xiii. 52: The disciples were filled with joy, and with the Holy Ghost. Acts xv. 8: God, which knoweth the hearts, bare them witness, giving them the Holy Ghost, even as he did unto us. Rom. viii. 11: If the Spirit of him that raised up Jesus from the dead dwell in you, he that raised up Christ from the dead shall also quicken your mortal bodies by his Spirit that dwelleth in you. 14: As many as are led by the Spirit of God, they are the sons of God. 23: Not only they, but ourselves also, which have the first-fruits of the Spirit. Rom. viii. 26: The Spirit also helpeth our infirmities: for we know not what we should pray for as we ought: but the

WHAT SAITH THE SCRIPTURE?

Spirit itself maketh intercession for us with groanings which cannot be uttered. 27: And he that searcheth the hearts knoweth what is the mind of the Spirit, because he maketh intercession for the saints according to the will of God. Rom. xv. 13: That ye may abound in hope, through the power of the Holy Ghost. 1 Cor. ii. 4: Not with enticing words of man's wisdom, but in demonstration of the Spirit and of power. 1 Cor. iii. 16: Know ye not that ye are the temple of God, and that the Spirit of God dwelleth in you? 1 Cor. xii. 4: Now there are diversities of gifts, but the same Spirit. 7: The manifestation of the Spirit is given to every man to profit withal. 9: To another faith by the same Spirit. 2 Cor. i. 22: Who hath also sealed us, and given the earnest of the

Spirit in our hearts. Gal. iv. 6: Because ye are sons, God hath sent forth the Spirit of his Son into your hearts, crying, Abba, Father. Gal. v. 5: We through the Spirit wait for the hope of righteousness by faith. 16: Walk in the Spirit, and ye shall not fulfil the lust of the flesh. 17: For the flesh lusteth against the Spirit, and the Spirit against the flesh: and these are contrary the one to the other; so that ye cannot do the things that ye would. 18: But if ye be led of the Spirit, ye are not under the law. 25: If we live in the Spirit, let us also walk in the Spirit. Gal. vi. 8: He that soweth to the Spirit shall of the Spirit reap life everlasting. Eph. i. 13, 14: After that ye believed, ye were sealed with that Holy Spirit of promise, which is the earnest of our inheritance until the redemption of the purchased possession, unto the praise of his glory. Eph. ii. 18: Through him we both have access by one Spirit unto the Father. 22: In whom ye also are builded together for a habitation of God through the Spirit. Eph. iv. 3: Endeavoring to keep the unity of the Spirit in the bond of peace. 4: There is one body, and one Spirit, even as ye are called in one hope of your calling. 30: The Holy Spirit of God, whereby ye are sealed unto the day of redemption. Eph. v. 9: The fruit of the Spirit is in all goodness and righteousness and truth. 18: Be filled with the Spirit. Eph. vi. 18: Praying always with all prayer and supplication in the Spirit. Phil. i. 19: This shall turn to my salvation through your prayer, and the supply of the Spirit of Jesus Christ. 1 Thess. i. 5: Our gospel came not unto you in word only, but also in power, and in the Holy Ghost. 6: Having received the word in much affliction, with joy of the Holy Ghost. 2 Tim. i. 7: God hath not given us the spirit of fear; but of power, and of love, and of a sound mind. 14: That good thing which was committed unto thee keep by the Holy Ghost which dwelleth in us. 1 John iii. 24: We know that he abideth in us, by the Spirit which he hath given us. 1 John iv. 2: Hereby know ye the Spirit of God: Every spirit that confesseth that Jesus Christ is come in the flesh is of God. 13: Hereby know we that we dwell in him, and he in us, because he hath given us of his Spirit. 1 John v. 6: It is the Spirit that beareth witness, because the Spirit is truth.

WHAT SAITH THE SCRIPTURE?

7: For there are three that bear record in heaven, the Father, the Word, and the Holy Ghost: and these three are one. 8: And there are three that bear witness in earth, the spirit, and the water, and the blood: and these three agree in one. Jude 20: Building up yourselves on your most holy faith, praying in the Holy Ghost. Rev. i. 4: Grace be unto you, and peace, from . . . the seven Spirits which are before his throne. Rev. xxii. 17: The Spirit and the bride say, Come.

**RECEIVED
YE THE
HOLY GHOST?**

**HOW MAY
I KNOW HIM?**

Cap II — *HOW MAY I KNOW HIM?*

"Afterward he brought me again unto the door of the house; and, behold, waters issued out from under the threshold of the house eastward."—Ezek. xlvii. 1.

NOTHING could be more important, in these days, than a clear discernment of the character and the work of the Holy Spirit. There is perhaps more ignorance concerning him than any other part of revealed truth. By many he is regarded as an undefinable influence. By many others he is supposed to come and go in a vague sort of way; now with the Christian and now absent from him; to-day with the church, to-morrow in some distant part of the world at work. All this is unscriptural, and must grieve him, who as certainly ABIDES with the true child of God as that Jesus died and arose again.

To know him aright has always meant POWER. To be ignorant of him has always meant confusion and ultimate defeat. The promise is, " Ye shall receive POWER, the Holy Ghost coming upon you." It is a possible thing for our creed to outrun our intelligence. We say again and again, " I believe in the Holy Ghost." Is it really true? With a single church believing in him we might move the world for God.

There is both ignorance and indifference concerning him, and the reason is most apparent. This is the " dispensation of the Spirit." It was ushered in at Pentecost. And Satan very well knows that so long as he can keep us in doubt as to the Spirit's work, or mystified as to his personality or presence, just so long he has nothing in us to fear. He cares not for your intellectual greatness—he can make a very snare of it—but he trembles when he sees one FILLED WITH THE HOLY GHOST.

Three propositions I would be glad to impress upon the mind, and in the light of them we shall study together the third person of the TRINITY: *First*, he has a personality. I might present many arguments to prove my statement. What stronger could there be than the words of our Lord himself?—" And I will pray the Father, and he shall give you another Comforter, that he may abide with you forever; even the Spirit of truth; whom the world cannot receive, because it seeth him not, neither knoweth him: but ye know him; for he dwelleth with you, and shall be in you." (John xiv. 16, 17.) Notice the word "another." This indicates that he is to take the place of Jesus himself. Could anything less than a person take the place of a person? Notice also the personal pronouns repeated as the Master speaks of the Comforter. Refer also to John xvi. 13, 14, where the pronouns are again repeated, and then read what Paul writes to the Ephesians: "Grieve not the Holy Spirit of God." (Eph. iv. 30.) You surely cannot grieve an influence, and this is all that some would have us believe him to be. Either they are mistaken or the Apostle is in error. Which position do you take? *Second*, this is his dispensation. This being true we need not *wait* to be filled with all his fullness. Some have thought this necessary, and have quoted the experience of the waiting disciples at Pentecost as a proof; but it is to be remembered that they were waiting for the coming in of a dispensation, while we live in it. The Holy Ghost is in no place said to have left the world after Pentecost. *Third*, he will fill us when we have fulfilled the conditions. These will be explained later, but in a word they are as follows: First, make an unconditional surrender to him, and let him abide in you, not because it is his work to do so, but because you have bidden him. Throw open every door of your nature, and give him undisputed possession. Second, believe his promise: "That we might receive the *promise* of the Spirit through *faith*." (Gal. iii. 14.) Do these things, then trust him to do his work. He is no respecter of persons. I had in a former parish a young Irishman; all would declare him to be ignorant, and he was; but God marvelously used him. This was the secret. With a heart burdened for the men of the city, I called together a few of the men of the church, and laying before them the plan I had in mind, told them first of all that we could do nothing without the "infilling of the Holy Ghost." When this had been explained I noticed this man leave the room. He did not return while the meeting was in session. When I sought him I found him in one of the lower rooms of the church, literally on his face before God. He was in prayer. I shall never forget his petition: " O God, I plead with thee for this blessing;" then, as if God were showing him what was in the way, he said: " My Father, I will give up every known sin, only I plead with thee for power;" and then, as if his individual sins were passing before him, he said again and again: " I will give them up; I will give them up." Then, without any emotion, he rose from his knees, turned his face heavenward, and simply said: "And now I claim the blessing." For the first time he became sensible of my presence, and with a shining countenance he reached out his hands to clasp mine.

You could feel the very presence of the Spirit as he said: " I have received him; I have received him." And I believe he had, for in the next few months he led more than sixty men into the kingdom of God. His whole life had been transformed. He is just now being set apart to preach the gospel. We may differ as to the terms we use, but of this one thing we are all persuaded: there is awaiting many of us an enlarging vision of the Holy Ghost; for many could say, as did the disciples at Ephesus, "We have not so much as heard whether there be any Holy Ghost." (Acts xix. 2.) Whether we speak of this vision as a baptism, an infilling, or an anointing, may he show us himself, for we seek him and not a mere experience; the latter may be a thing of the moment, the former abides forever. (John xiv. 16.)

The forty-seventh chapter of Ezekiel gives to me a beautiful figure of what the Holy Spirit is, and the work he does. There is something in the source of the river, something in the direction in which it runs, something in its increasing depth as it nears the sea, and something in its fruited banks to lead us to him of whom we study. First have in mind the temple from which the river flows. It is suggestive. As you know, the temple in the Old Testament was divided into three main parts: first, the outer court, into which any child of Israel might make his way; second, the holy place, where only the white-robed priests might walk to and fro; and third, the holy of holies, where only the high priest might go, and that but once a year. This Old Testament temple typifies the temple of which Paul speaks in the New Testament: " Know ye not that ye are the temple of God, and that the Spirit of God dwelleth in you?" (1 Cor. iii. 16.) So the New Testament temple is yourself: "Which temple ye are." (1 Cor. iii. 17.) There is likewise a threefold division here. There is first the outer court, which corresponds to the body; the second court is the soul, the third court is the spirit. There are some people who never live beyond the outer court; but such do not understand what it is to live. It is a possible thing for the body to be controlled, or, at least, influenced by the Spirit, for we read: " He that raised up Christ from the dead shall also quicken your mortal bodies by his Spirit that dwelleth in you." (Rom. viii. 11.) It is apparent to all that he works in the soul, that is, the real self, the "ego." Here also the Spirit manifests himself, for we read: "Seeing ye have purified your souls in obeying the truth through the Spirit." (1 Peter i. 22.) But all must be aware that there are experiences deeper than the soul, and thus we are led to the spirit; this is the "holy of holies." It has been called "the secret place of the Most High." It is the place where God dwells. And here the Spirit works, for we read: "For ye are bought with a price: therefore glorify God in your body, and in your spirit, which are God's." (1 Cor. vi. 20.) And again: "The Spirit himself beareth witness with our spirit, that we are the children of God." (Rom. viii. 16.) And just as in the chapter to which reference has been made the sanctuary was so filled with the water that it rushed out by the way of the altar eastward, so we may be " filled with the Spirit," and so filled that there shall not only be communion, that is, for ourselves, but there may be the manifestation of power to others, illustrated in the flowing river. Our whole nature, body, soul, and spirit, may be swayed by his presence. If the temple pictures the real self, the man of to-day, then the water must stand for something. In the light of the Word of God, what would you say? I am sure we are making no mistake when we say that the water typifies the Holy Ghost. We surely have the right to say as much, for Jesus himself said it. Speaking to the woman of Samaria he said: "But whosoever drinketh of the water that I shall give him shall never thirst; but the water that I shall give him shall be in him a well of water springing up into everlasting life." (John iv. 14.) This is the "indwelling Spirit." But at the last day of the feast he made it still plainer when he said: "He that believeth on me, as the Scripture hath said, out of his belly shall flow rivers of living water. (But this spake he of the Spirit, which they that believe on him should receive: for the Holy Ghost was not yet given; because that Jesus was not yet glorified." (John vii. 38, 39.) This is the river flowing out from the sanctuary, running through the desert, healing the waters of the sea of life.

God often speaks to us by means of figures or types. This is an illustration. It may be both interesting and profitable to present other emblems of the Spirit, for each will come to us with a particular lesson.

I. THE WIND.

Sometimes he is spoken of under the figure of the wind, and this is generally when we would present his quickening, powerful, penetrating influence. There are many things about it which may be mentioned, all of which help us to understand the work of the Spirit the better. *First, the wind is invisible:* "The wind bloweth where it listeth, and thou hearest the sound thereof, but thou canst not tell whence it cometh, and whither it goeth: so is every one that is born of the

Spirit." (John iii. 8.) To my mind this beautifully presents to us one of the chief traits of the Spirit. He came not to draw attention to himself, but to the Son. We are told in another place concerning the Son, that he "made himself of no reputation, and took upon himself the form of a servant, and was made in the likeness of men." (Phil. ii. 7.) But herein was the love of the Spirit made manifest, for he came into the world without even the form of a servant. Suppose he had become incarnate, would there not have been a temptation to forget the incarnate Son in the contemplation of the incarnate Spirit? The Holy Ghost always magnifies the Lord Jesus Christ, *just as the river from the sanctuary ran eastward. Second, the wind is penetrating.* It is said

RECEIVED YE THE HOLY GHOST?

that "nature abhors a vacuum." This is true, but it is likewise true that the Spirit abhors a vacuum, and we may rest assured that just as soon as the room is made for him he will fill us to overflowing. He abides with us now, but we may never feel the blessedness of his presence till we have forsaken all sin, surrendered all selfishness; for selfishness, sin, and worldliness cannot possess the child of God, if we would have the Spirit in his fullness. *Third, the wind is powerful.* A perfect illustration is found in the valley of dry bones. The valley was filled with the bones of the dead when the word of the Lord came to his servant to prophesy. John McNeil says he can imagine that Ezekiel looked down and he was afraid to say "Yes"; he looked up and he was afraid to say "No"; and so he answered, "O Lord God, thou knowest." "So I prophesied as I was commanded: and as I prophesied, there was a noise, and behold a shaking, and the bones came together, bone to bone. And when I beheld, lo, the sinews and the flesh came up upon them, and the skin covered them above: but there was no breath in them. Then he said unto me, Prophesy unto the wind, prophesy, son of man, and say to the wind, Thus saith the Lord God; Come from the four winds, O breath, and breathe upon these slain, that they may live. So I prophesied as he commanded me, and the breath came into them, and they lived, and stood up upon their feet, an exceeding great army." (Ezek. xxxvii. 7–10.) Surely this is a picture of all that the church might be, if we were, as individuals, " filled with the Spirit."

II. THE DOVE.

The dove is an emblem of the Holy Spirit, telling of his loving, tender, comforting work. This, of all the family of birds, is the most lovely. Its affection for its mate is almost pathetic. In its choice of a home, in the company it keeps, in its food, as well as in its very self, it is a beautiful picture of much that the Spirit may be in us. It is very helpful to me to know that when we receive him fully we become partakers of his nature. One could not be petulant, impatient, censorious, disagreeable, and be filled with his fullness. For when of his fullness we have received, we have "grace for grace," and what can this mean but a duplication of graces? (John i. 16.) In Paul's letter to the Galatians we read: "But the *fruit* of the Spirit is love, joy, peace, long-suffering, gentleness, goodness, faith, meekness, temperance: against such there is no law." (Gal. v. 22, 23.) You will notice that the word "fruit" is used in the singular number, and the inference must be that when we give ourselves up to the Spirit we have, not one of these graces, but all of them. First, the dove is a *patient* bird. Surely here it brings us a lesson of the Spirit. We have grieved him a thousand times, and yet he is the same tender, patient Spirit. As another has said: "Look at the way he is grieved." "Let no corrupt communication proceed out of your mouth, but that which is good to the use of edifying, that it may minister grace to the hearers. And grieve not the Holy Spirit of God, whereby ye are sealed unto the day of redemption. Let all bitterness, and wrath, and anger, and clamor, and evil speaking, be put away from you, with all malice: and be ye kind one to another, tender-hearted, forgiving one another, even as God for Christ's sake hath forgiven you." (Eph. iv. 29–32.) Compare this with the malice and evil speaking and censoriousness and slander that are notoriously common among professing Christians: we no longer wonder that the Holy Spirit is grieved. Every idle word, every unkind expression, every unholy thought grieves him, yet he tarries, waiting, yearning to fill us with his blessed presence and power. Second, the dove is a *loving* bird. We are well acquainted with the thought that God the Father loves us, and all must be sensible of the love of the Son, but of the love of the Spirit we are not so well informed. Yet Paul writes: "Now I beseech you, brethren, for the Lord Jesus Christ's sake, and for the love of the Spirit, that ye strive together with me in your prayers to God for me." (Rom. xv. 30.) "The love of the Spirit for every sinner who trusts in Christ for salvation can be measured only by the infinite and eternal love of the Father, and by the intense, self-sacrificing, boundless, and unchanging love of the Son." The first mention of the Spirit in the Old Testament suggests his love. We read: "And the Spirit moved upon the face of the waters." (Gen. i. 2.) The word "moved" in the Hebrew is literally "brooded," giving us the figure of the mother-bird hovering over her young; and if the word is studied more closely, it means to be "tremulous with love." This is the first picture, and he is "the same yesterday, to-day, and forever." To be "filled with the Spirit" thus means to be filled with this spirit. What a transformation it would mean to the individual and to the church! It would mean the reclaiming of the lost. In Isaiah we read: "But thou hast in love to my soul delivered it from the pit of corruption" (Isa. xxxviii. 17), and in the margin you read that it means "thou hast loved up my soul from the pit." It would mean the winning of souls.

HOW MAY I KNOW HIM?

It may be interesting to know that one of the first Salvation Army converts was thus won in France. Miss Booth had been singing and speaking for weeks. The people crowded around her only for the purpose of ridicule. At last, one evening when she had told her story with all the pathos with which she was capable, she went down from the platform and pushed her way through the crowd till she reached a fallen girl sitting in the rear of the room. She threw her arms about her neck and kissed her first upon one cheek, then upon the other, and she said as she did so, "My dear sister, I would that I could love you into the kingdom." The girl looked up in a startled way; pure lips like those had not touched her cheeks in many a day. She burst into tears. Miss Booth led her sobbing to the penitent form, where with true repentance she cried out for forgiveness. God saved her and she has been a good soldier ever since. Oh, that the church might be filled with this spirit!

> "Come, Holy Spirit, heavenly Dove,
> With all thy quickening powers:
> Come, shed abroad a Saviour's love,
> And that shall kindle ours."

III. THE OIL.

When God would reveal to us the healing, comforting, illuminating, and consecrating influences of the Spirit, he directs our minds to the oil, which shadows forth these characteristics. In a part of the description of the ancient tabernacle you read this sentence: "Oil for the light." (Ex. xxxv. 8.) This suggests the illustration another has used,

HOW MAY I KNOW HIM?

letting the oil represent the Spirit, the wick the Christian, and the light stand for the result of the union of the two. There may be an abundance of oil and a plentiful supply of wick—there cannot be light until the two are brought together. I know the Spirit abides in us, and will forever, but there can never be a manifestation of his power till by the consent of our wills he has undisputed possession. The two may be brought together, and for a time the light is brilliant, but in a little while it is dim and flickering, and every housekeeper can understand the difficulty— the wick has become incrusted and must be trimmed. It is not enough for us to be right with God to-day, that we may have a manifestation of his power—we must KEEP RIGHT. The secret may be

RECEIVED YE THE HOLY GHOST?

found in one sentence: "Confess your sins instantly." Even if the oil and the wick be brought together, there may be still little or no light, and the difficulty is, that there is a knot in the wick. It is not enough that the Spirit abide with us—this he does. The heart must be right in the sight of God. This was the difficulty with Simon the sorcerer. (Acts viii. 9–13.) When he tried to purchase with money the power of the Holy Ghost, he failed, because his heart was not right. We have, however, the privilege of believing that when the heart is right we have the very fullness of God himself. He is sometimes said to be the "oil to make the face shine." (Ps. civ. 15.) It is not possible to be filled with the Holy Ghost and then simply delight in the fact ourselves. God

HOW MAY I KNOW HIM?

never bestows such a gift that we may consume it upon our own lusts. He is the outflowing river, and also reveals himself in the shining countenance. He is called the "oil of gladness." "Therefore God, thy God, hath anointed thee with the oil of gladness above thy fellows." (Ps. xlv. 7.) It is a most comforting thought that Satan cannot rob us of our life, for that is "hid with Christ in God." But he may deprive us of our JOY. It has been said that it is the work of Christ to bring us to heaven, but it is the work of the Spirit to bring heaven to us now. The Psalmist tells us: "In thy presence is fullness of joy" (Ps. xvi. 11); and since it is the work of the Spirit to lead us into God's presence, that means just one thing, namely, HEAVEN.

IV. THE WATER.

Water is typical of many things in the Bible. Sometimes it stands for judgment, sometimes for the Bible itself; but most frequently for the Holy Ghost does it stand as a type. Very many things may be said of the water, and the same things apply to the Holy Spirit.

First, the water is *free*. We may have it without money and without price. There is no truer thought than this about the Spirit. To rich or poor, to wise or ignorant, he will come with all his fullness. "By grace are we saved," and "by grace are we filled with his blessed presence." Second, the water is *refreshing*. "He leadeth me beside the still waters." (Ps. xxiii. 2.) When

HOW MAY I KNOW HIM?

the journey is long, and the way dusty and hard to travel, and we are worn and weary, what is more refreshing than the springs of water? We stoop to drink and push out on our way rejoicing. All that the water is to the traveler, yea, a thousand times more, the Spirit of God is to the weary ones. The water in us is a well "springing up." It comes from the throne, it rises again to its source, for water always seeks its own level; and here is the thought of communion that is always refreshing. The water flowing out from us is a river, and that does not flow for itself, but for others. Thus the Spirit always leads us. And who has not found that in living for others he has made his own way brighter and his own path easier to travel? What is this but the very best of refreshment? Third, the water is *cleansing*. I am well aware that it is the work of the blood of Jesus Christ to "cleanse from all sin," but it is the work of the Spirit to bring that work to remembrance, so we may speak of him as cleansing. The word "cleansing" has several different meanings in the Word of God. Sometimes it is *katharos*, which means to "clear up." This must have been in Paul's mind when he said: "Be careful for nothing; but in everything by prayer and supplication with thanksgiving let your requests be made known unto God. And the peace of God, which passeth all understanding, shall keep your hearts and minds through Christ Jesus." (Phil. iv. 6, 7.) Careful for nothing, prayerful for everything, thankful for anything, as another has said. Sometimes it is *katharizo*, which means to "make clean"; and I am glad to know that this the Spirit of God surely does. We are told to keep ourselves "unspotted from the world." That would be most difficult were it not for the presence of the Spirit: with him it is easy. While in the mountains of Colorado, I noticed the miners going into the mine at the beginning of their "shifts"—their hands and faces were clean as they could make them; but at the end of the "shifts" it would be difficult to tell whether they were by nature black or white, and yet there was one part of the face which was just as clean as when they entered the mine: that was the ball of the eye; and that not because no impurities had touched it, for the mine was filled with such, but because there is a little tear-gland which keeps working all the time, and when the least speck touches the eye it washes it away. We are in the midst of sin and uncleanness in this world, but we may be kept clean every whit if we be only "filled with the Spirit." Keep in mind this river from the sanctuary, its source, its marvelous influence for good as it flows, and, not the least of all, keep in mind the direction in which it flowed. It will bear us on in our study till we are in the very "secret of his presence."

**RECEIVED
YE THE
HOLY GHOST?**

**HOW MAY
I RECEIVE HIM?**

Cap III   *HOW MAY I RECEIVE HIM?*

"That we might receive the promise of the Spirit through faith."—Gal. iii. 14.

THE Apostle Paul in his journeyings had come to Ephesus and found there a company of twelve men who were trying in a rude way to lead a holy life. They were John's disciples. They had been instructed by him in the doctrine of repentance, and it is supposed that they were members of the church of Corinth. Possibly because there was evidently something lacking in their testimony, or, as others have supposed, because they may have been denying the power of God in their lives or conversation, the Apostle puts to them the question, "Did ye receive the Holy Ghost when ye believed? And they said unto him, Nay, we did not so much as hear whether the Holy Ghost was." (Acts xix. 2, R. V.) It is not for a moment to be supposed that they were ignorant of the existence of the Spirit, for they were Jews, and their Scriptures teemed with references to his work. Then, too, they must have heard John speak of him. What they meant, undoubtedly, was that they had not heard of him as the abiding Comforter; and in this they were like many of the church-members of to-day. When Jesus ascended the Spirit came. It was his

HOW MAY I RECEIVE HIM?

work, as it is now, to take up his abode in the hearts of believers. David might pray, "Take not thy Holy Spirit from me" (Ps. li. 11), but it would be a betrayal of ignorance for the child of God to offer such a petition to-day. There is not a thought in the New Testament suggesting that we "may grieve him away." What a difference there is between the Old Testament picture of the Spirit and the New Testament view of him! There he is represented as having his part in the work of creation: "And the Spirit of God moved upon the face of the waters." (Gen. i. 2.) He is there made known as the source of deliverance for his people: "And the Spirit of the Lord came upon him, and he judged Israel, and went out to war." (Judges iii. 10.) He was then, as now, the spring of all strength and courage: "And the Spirit of the Lord came mightily upon him, and he rent him as he would have rent a kid." (Judges xiv. 6.) But in the New Testament he is called the "Comforter": "And I will pray the Father, and he shall give you another Comforter." (John xiv. 16.) He is called the Teacher or Guide: "When the Spirit of truth is come, he will guide you into all truth." (John xvi. 13.)

There is an illustration of this truth in the Old Testament, which another has used. In the days of the flood, when Noah opened the window of the ark, the little dove flew over the waters, and finding no place to rest the sole of its foot, it came back again to the outstretched hand. He let it go

HOW MAY I RECEIVE HIM?

forth a second time. Flying hither and thither, it came back with an olive leaf in its mouth. He let it go yet the third time, and it found a resting-place for the sole of its foot, and it returned no more forever. The dove generally typifies the Spirit. In this case it at least tells a story of his coming. He came in the Old Testament, breathing upon Moses, burning in Isaiah, speaking through the lips of Abraham, but in the old dispensation he is not said to abide. He came when Jesus was crucified, and plucked, as it were, the olive leaf of peace from the cross (for the olive is the symbol of peace), and bore it back to the presence of God, saying, " Peace hath been made in the death of the Son." But he came the third time at Pentecost, with a rushing sound as of a mighty wind, and from that day to this he has never gone back. He has found his abiding-place in the hearts of believers.

It is interesting to notice how he is manifested, and how his coming is described. Sometimes he is represented as "clothing" his chosen ones, as, for example: "Tarry ye in the city of Jerusalem, until ye be endued with power from on high." (Luke xxiv. 49.) The word translated "endued" is elsewhere rendered "clothed." He is also represented as "poured out," to indicate his freeness: "Behold, I will pour out my spirit unto you." (Prov. i. 23.) He is represented as "filling," or taking complete possession of. It was predicted of John the Baptist, "He shall be filled with the Holy Ghost."

HOW MAY I RECEIVE HIM?

And to be "filled with the Spirit" is far more a scriptural expression than to be "baptized with the Holy Ghost." John the Baptist, Elizabeth, Zacharias, Jesus, Stephen, Barnabas, and Paul were all "filled with the Spirit," and we are told to be "filled with the Spirit." (Eph. v. 18.) There is a distinction here well worth our consideration. To be "baptized with the Spirit" may mean a pentecostal experience, a great rush of feeling, a change as great in the believer as the change from night to day. Not many people have such an experience, and for that reason multitudes are deprived of the real blessing of the Spirit's presence. To be "filled with the Spirit" may be almost the opposite of such an experience as that referred to. Mr. Meyer says that you can fill a cistern with water just as surely by letting little drops of water fall into it as by pouring in great hogsheads of water.

There are really two parts to the receiving of the Holy Ghost. First of all there is the baptism of the Spirit, as found in 1 Corinthians xii. 12, 13: "For as the body is one, and hath many members, and all the members of that body, being many, are one body: so also is Christ. For by one Spirit are we all *baptized* into one body, whether we be Jews or Gentiles, whether we be bond or free; and have been all made to drink into one Spirit." The second part is described in Acts i. 8: "But ye shall receive power, after that the Holy Ghost is come upon you: and ye shall be witnesses unto me both in Jerusalem, and in all Judea, and in Samaria, and unto the uttermost part of the earth." This is power, and depends upon one's moral condition. According to this outline, then, every child of God has received the baptism of the Spirit; he is also, because of this, a member of the body of Christ. This experience can never be repeated; so, then, it is unscriptural for the Christian to be talking about the baptism of the Holy Ghost when he has already received it: but he may be filled with the Spirit and then, because of his moral condition, lose the power of the Spirit, as we find the disciples doing. They were filled in the first chapter of Acts, and in the fourth chapter of Acts, thirty-first verse, it is said again that "they were all filled with the Holy Ghost, and they spake the word of God with boldness." If you will study the second and third chapters, you will find that the disciples had lack of courage, and for that very reason had lost their blessing; but when the Spirit came upon them again, they became possessed of the very thing in which they had been lacking. There is, therefore, one baptism, many fillings. The Holy Ghost as certainly abides in us as that Jesus Christ stands to-day at the right hand of the Father. We need only to remove the hindrances in order that he may manifest his power; so, therefore, "Take ye away the stone." I am persuaded that to be "filled with the Spirit" we must make a complete and definite surrender and then trust him to do his work. He will, doubtless, begin in some little way to manifest his presence, just as it were drop by

HOW MAY I RECEIVE HIM?

drop. To-day a new pathos in the voice, to-morrow a new touch of the hand, and so on day by day, till his presence in all its fullness will be a blessed reality. The first step, however, in this blessing, as the first step into the "life of the eternal," is a step of faith. I used to be greatly troubled by the recitation of personal experiences in many of the public meetings. One would say, "I was converted such a year;" another, such a month; another, such a day or hour; and to me it was discouraging, for I could not tell the year, much less the day. But I am distressed about it no longer, and for two reasons: First, I should know I was living physically even if I did not know my birthday, and I may know that I am living spiritually even though I do not know when I "passed from death into life." My second reason is found in the fact that I have a better experience: I have had my eyes opened to the truth of the Spirit; and if you will allow me to choose between the man who has had a definite experience in conversion, and knows little of the Holy Ghost, and the man who may be uncertain as to the time of his conversion, but knows about the third person of the Trinity, I will choose the latter every time, for I am certain that I may be a Christian and not know when I crossed the line, but I cannot be a Christian with an experience of power until I know something definite about the Holy Ghost.

What vague ideas and views we have concerning him! We think of him as coming and going, with us to-day, away

HOW MAY I RECEIVE HIM?

from us to-morrow. We pray for his outpouring. We cry out in sermon, in song, and in prayer, "Come, Holy Ghost," as if he were still in the skies, when the fact is that he abides with us ALWAYS and is nearer to us than our right hand. He may not always be manifesting his power, but that is because we have placed some hindrance in the way. In a sense, there is a twofold bestowal of the Spirit, but it is like this, quoting from Dr. James H. Brooks in his work on the Holy Spirit: "We are told that on the evening of the same day that our Lord arose from the grave, 'when the doors were shut where the disciples were assembled for fear of the Jews, came Jesus and stood in the midst, and saith unto them, Peace be unto you. And when he had so said, he showed unto them his hands and his side. Then were the disciples glad, when they saw the Lord. Then said Jesus to them again, Peace be unto you: as my Father hath sent me, even so send I you. And when he had said this, he breathed on them, and saith unto them, Receive ye the Holy Ghost.' (John xx. 19–22.) No one can imagine that these solemn words were uttered in vain, or that the disciples did not then receive the Holy Ghost. It makes the language and action of our risen Lord all the more significant when we remember that this is the only place in the New Testament where the word rendered 'breathed' is found, and that the Saviour never elsewhere is said to breathe on any one." The other was the bestowal of the Spirit at Pentecost, when they were qualified

HOW MAY I RECEIVE HIM?

as witnesses. Hence there is a twofold bestowal of the Spirit: one secret and inward, within closed doors as it were; the other open and outward in its manifestations. The former is never repeated; the latter is repeated over and over according to the measure of our faith and of our desire. The former was Christ's gift to his servants; it was a special blessing for a special purpose. The latter was in fulfilment of the promise, "Ye shall receive power, after that the Holy Ghost is come upon you: and ye shall be witnesses unto me." (Acts i. 8.)

One word needs to be sounded over and over again if we are to be the recipients of this blessing. That word is "surrender." The very moment we have fulfilled this condition then rest assured that he will begin the manifestation of himself. We are not to suppose that we may mark out the channel in which he is to run, for the WILL must be given up in this as in other things. It is generally supposed, however, that to be filled with the Spirit always means power from the human standpoint, and this is anything but true. It always means power; but power in the estimation of God may mean defeat in the thought of men. It is to be remembered that Peter was "filled with the Holy Ghost," and preached the sermon at Pentecost, while Stephen was "filled with the Holy Ghost," and was stoned to death: one was as great a victory in the sight of God as the other.

Not infrequently the children of God go mourning after this blessing and find

HOW MAY I RECEIVE HIM?

it not, and for the reason that they are seeking the consciousness of the blessing rather than the Spirit himself. We have nothing to do with the consciousness: we are to have faith in God, believing in the indwelling Spirit when with great emotion and much enthusiasm we are working, as well as when without either we do his bidding. Consciousness of power may be a very dangerous thing. There is hardly an old horse with which we are familiar which we would be willing to drive if that horse were conscious of his power. He could break away from us in an instant—but he is not conscious. We have the consciousness, and he has the power, and so we guide him whithersoever we will. Let us just believe God, and let him be conscious of all that we may accomplish. It is ours just to be submissive.

I. HOW MAY I RECEIVE HIM?

First. One of the most important steps with which I am familiar is this: do not seek to know him, first of all, that you might teach or preach with power. This is not the way to the blessing. Again, do not seek to know him that you may have the peace of which others have spoken who have known him in all his fullness. This is not the first step. But rather, bid him abide in you, that, first of all, HE MAY HAVE POWER OVER YOURSELF. He is the fire, and will, if allowed, burn out the dross. He is the water, and he will keep the temple clean. Then only may we expect to be

HOW MAY I RECEIVE HIM?

used. Mr. Moody has so many times said: "God does not seek silver vessels, and he does not require gold ones for his service, but he must have clean ones."

Second. The second step has already been indicated. It is this: SURRENDER FULLY. To give up ninety-nine parts of the nature and withhold the hundredth is to put a hindrance in the way of the blessing. If a contagious disease had been raging in a certain house, and you had a desire to live in the house, you know that you would not do it until every room had been purified. If every room but one had been fumigated, and that the smallest room, you know that you would not occupy the house. Nor will the Holy Spirit work with power in the life till it has all been surrendered to him, till it has all been made clean by true confession: then make ready for the blessing which God has promised. I can remember when God opened my eyes to this truth. I had been struggling for five years, I had had visions of his power and glimpses of what I might be if I were "filled with the Spirit," but all this time, like the disciples at Ephesus, there was a great lacking. At last I reached the place where I felt that I was willing to make the surrender. I reached it by the path marked out by Mr. Meyer when he said: "If you are not ready to surrender everything to God, are you ready to say, 'I am willing to be made willing about everything'?" That seemed easy, and alone before God I simply said, "I am willing." Then he made the way easy. He brought before me my ambition, then my personal ease, then my home, then other things came to me, and I simply said, " I will give them up." And last of all my "will" was surrendered about everything. Then without any emotion, for, as Mr. Meyer said, it was " faith without emotion," I said, " My Father, I now claim from thee the infilling of the Holy Ghost." From that moment to this he has been a living reality. I never knew what it was to love my family before, I question if they ever knew what it was to love me, although we had called ourselves happy in the love of each other. I never knew what it was to study the Bible before, and why should I? For had I not just then found the key? I never knew what it was to preach before. "Old things are passed away;" in my Christian experience, "behold, all things are become new."

Third. The third step is found in Paul's letter to the Galatians, where he says: "That we might receive the promise of the Spirit through faith." (Gal. iii. 14.) You will notice that it does not say, "That we might receive the Spirit through faith." It is often so quoted. This would be unscriptural, for we have the Spirit. He is with us to abide forever. It is just to believe his word; and the third step is one of FAITH. We say to the man seeking Christ, and yet who hesitates because he is without feeling —we say to him, "It is faith first, then feeling after;" and so we say to all who seek the infilling of the Holy Ghost, "Receive the promise by faith."

HOW MAY I RECEIVE HIM?

These steps do not of necessity follow in logical order, for the last may be first if one so desires; but the next step suggested would be this: keep your eyes fixed upon Christ. There is an Old Testament illustration of this. When Elijah and Elisha were journeying toward the place of the translation, you will remember that the people came out at Bethel, Gilgal, and other places, and entreated Elisha to tarry with them for a season, and Elijah said, "Tarry, I pray thee, here." (2 Kings ii. 6.) "And he said, As the Lord liveth, and as thy soul liveth, I will not leave thee." (2 Kings ii. 6.) "And it came to pass, when they were gone over, that Elijah said unto Elisha, Ask what I shall do for thee, before I be taken away from thee.

And Elisha said, I pray thee, let a double portion of thy spirit be upon me. And he said, Thou hast asked a hard thing: nevertheless, if thou see me when I am taken from thee, it shall be so unto thee; but if not, it shall not be so." (2 Kings ii. 9, 10.) Suddenly, as they talked, the chariot of fire appeared, and Elijah became a passenger. I suppose Elisha was too greatly surprised to speak at first; then he cried out, "My father, my father, the chariot of Israel, and the horsemen thereof." (2 Kings ii. 12.) And Elijah dropped upon him, I imagine, the old mantle, for it is said that he took it up. Suppose he had wrapped it around him, saying, "How comfortable it is!" what benefit would it have been? But he did not do this. He had his reward when the old mantle fell upon him. He simply stood on the banks of the Jordan and used the mantle as his master had used it, and the waters parted as before. We are given the Spirit not that we may consume him upon our own lusts, but in order that we may be in this world as Jesus himself. Do you remember his words, " Verily, verily, I say unto you, He that believeth on me, the works that I do shall he do also; and greater works than these shall he do; because I go unto my Father"? (John xiv. 12.) What is this but Elijah and Elisha again? Here is the secret of it all: KEEP YOUR EYES FIXED ON A TAKEN-UP MASTER. Elisha had the spirit of his master before. I suppose he had followed him so closely that he had absorbed the very spirit of Elijah; but it was the double portion he was seeking, and that he received. So it is with us if we are in Christ: we have the indwelling Spirit; but we need, and we must have, the double portion, and this comes with a knowledge of the Spirit, which every one may have in Christ.

II. SUGGESTIONS.

It may be helpful to ask the question, "Why have I not received him?" This may be for many reasons.

First. It may be because we have disobeyed some clear command of the Master: if at any time in the past we have broken a thread in the weaving of a garment, we need not expect to know about the fullness of the Spirit until we have made the past right with God. If it was an unkind word spoken, an inconsistent action which caused another to stumble or fall, if it is some unforgiven sin, then make it right; and then, too, it is not enough to get right, as we often hear, but we must keep right. And there is no way by which this may be so easily accomplished as just to be quick to obey God's least commands. Be very sensitive to his leadings and teachings; offer this prayer of David's: " Search me, O God, and know my heart: try me, and know my thoughts: and see if there be any wicked way in me, and lead me in the way everlasting." (Ps. cxxxix. 23, 24.)

Second. The second suggestion may be embraced with the first, but it is made distinct, at least for the sake of emphasis. It may be that the difficulty is found in the fact that you have not confessed your sin. In a western city

RECEIVED YE THE HOLY GHOST?

a gentleman approached the evangelist laboring in the city with this question: "Can you tell me why it is that I have no power in my Christian life? I have a class of men in the Sunday-school, and have had for three years, and have never been able to lead one of them to Christ." The evangelist replied, "It may be because your heart is not right with God, and that you are hiding some sin." The man's face became pale, and then in the secrecy of the minister's room he made his confession: "Twelve years ago I was a clerk in a mercantile establishment in the city of P———. One night in balancing my books I had two hundred dollars for which I could not account; my books were balanced, but the money was there. The books balanced the next day and the next week, and the money was still not accounted for. Then the devil came to me to say, 'Use it; no one will ever know it, and you can put it back.' God pity me! I took it, and all these years I have had it. Here it is," he said, handing it to the evangelist. " I cannot take it," he said; "you will have to make restitution." The man sprang to his feet, exclaiming: " I can never do it. I have a position now worth twenty thousand dollars a year to me, and I should lose it if I were even suspected of being dishonest in the past." " It is either restitution or no power," said the evangelist. The man was still for a moment; then, rising to his feet, he exclaimed, " I will do it if I die." He made his way to the city where the wrong had been committed, into the private office of the man against whom he had sinned, and made confession. The Christian merchant listened to his words; then, rising, he closed the door of the office, and said, "Let us pray about it." They fell on their knees, and when the prayer was offered the merchant said to him: "Go back to your work, and God's blessing go with you. I forgive you just as freely as he does." The man came back to his home with his face shining. The next Sunday he sat down before his class to tell them of Christ. He said to them: "I never knew till this week why it was that I could not get you for Christ. I have now found out. It was because I was not right myself." Then, turning to his class, he made such a plea as he had never made before, and with the result that every member of his class accepted

HOW MAY I RECEIVE HIM?

Christ as Saviour, and a few Sundays after joined the church of which he was a member. It is very easy to understand why. He had simply gotten right with God, and then the Spirit, who had been abiding in him all the time, used him; and that is always the Spirit's way.

Third. Again, it may be that we have too little communion with God in his Word. Have you not always noticed that when one knew his Bible he knew the Spirit well? It is the poverty of the knowledge of the Word of God that makes us poor in our understanding of the Spirit. He inspired holy men of old to write the Book. Why should we not know him if we know his thought? When one of our Christian philanthropists was presiding, a number of years ago, at a great Peace Congress in

RECEIVED YE THE HOLY GHOST?

Washington, in the midst of their deliberations a company of Indians came in. They were asked to speak, and through an interpreter an old chief made the following remarks: "We have come here to see the Great Father, the President. We have come to ask him to help our people." And then looking about on the crowd assembled, he said: "Our people are not like yours, our women and children are not like yours, our homes are not like yours. Can you tell the Indian," he said, " what medicine he must take to make him right?" Then Major-General O. O. Howard, who was a member of the congress, the man who wears an empty coat-sleeve to the honor of his country, the man who is a loyal soldier of Christ as well, sprang to the speaker's desk, and with his one arm

HOW MAY I RECEIVE HIM?

raised aloft the Bible, exclaiming, while every one was thrilled: " Mr. Speaker, tell him this is the Good Medicine." And it is. It is the medicine to make right the world's wrongs; it is the medicine to purify the heart; and to know this is to know the Spirit, while to know the Spirit is POWER.

RECEIVED YE THE HOLY GHOST?

WHAT OF THE RESULT?

Cap IV — *WHAT OF THE RESULT?*

"But ye shall receive power, after that the Holy Ghost is come upon you: and ye shall be witnesses unto me both in Jerusalem, and in all Judea, and in Samaria, and unto the uttermost part of the earth."
—Acts i. 8.

REFERRING again to the river from the sanctuary, we get the best answer to this question. The river ran into the desert. The Spirit of God always leads us into the world, that we may go to the lost and tell them of life, bidding them in the name of Christ and on the authority of the Word and by the power of the Spirit to believe in him, that their position may be changed —a good illustration of which is Mephibosheth. He dwelt at Lo-debar (which means "the place of no pasture"), but through the kindness of David, for Jonathan's sake, he is brought to the king's table that he may have plenty. The river was healing, for we read that, running into the sea, the waters thereof were healed. The river was life-giving: "And it shall come to pass, that everything that liveth, which moveth, whithersoever the rivers shall come, shall live." (Ezek. xlvii. 9.) It is fruit-producing and food-providing. What a river it was! But there was one thing it could not do, namely, change the marshy places: "But the miry places thereof and the marshes thereof shall

WHAT OF THE RESULT?

not be healed; they shall be given to salt." (Ezek. xlvii. 11.) The Spirit does not come to improve man's carnal nature. "That which is born of the flesh is flesh," and always will be. But all that the river does, as described above, we may have repeated in our lives. Our position is "in the world, but not of it." We have had placed in our keeping for wounded hearts the very balm of Gilead. We have the words of eternal life, we have the very bread of heaven—in fact, we have all things in Christ. There would be a marvelous change in the church as well as in the individual if only we were "filled with the Spirit." We have to-day in the church men enough, and they have money enough, and, humanly speaking, we have power enough to put to flight the enemy, if only we were "filled with the Holy Ghost."

I have a friend in New York City, a most remarkable woman. She has turned away from her social position, given up, for the time being, her home, with the full consent of her family, and devotes all her time and her strength to the rescuing of "fallen girls." She has literally prayed up the Door of Hope, an institution which is a refuge for all such; and there is never a night so dark or so long but the doors of this home are open for the wanderer. One night at midnight, leaving her home, going out on an expedition through the slums of New York, she held in her hand a beautiful pink rose. She said to one of her friends, "I will give this rose to the vilest girl I meet in my wanderings."

WHAT OF THE RESULT?

She made her way to Mulberry Street, a place which is a veritable hell. It is the place where men and women go when all hope has fled from them and they are ready to throw themselves into perdition. In one of the subcellars, surrounded by some of New York's worst characters, was the girl whom Mrs. Whittemore, in her mind, had been seeking. This was the description she gave of her: her hair was torn out as if she had been in a recent brawl, as they found out afterward she had; her face bore the marks of sin; her clothing hung in rags from her poor, thin shoulders; her feet were pressing their way through her old shoes; her eyes were as blue as the sky, and for that reason she was called by her companions "Blue Bird." As my friend stood looking at her, she told me that the vilest profanity she had ever heard was falling from her lips. She pushed her way through the crowd of men, and placed in the girl's hand the pink rose, saying as she did so: "My dear, if ever in your life you want a friend, come to the Door of Hope, and I will be a mother to you." The girl at once replied, "I'm too sinful to be saved or helped." But Mrs. Whittemore left her that night with the prayer that she might come. Several days after, just as my friend was going into the Door of Hope, she found Blue Bird, looking more miserable than before. The first thought was one of discouragement, and the second almost a determination to put her out into the street, for it did seem impossible, even with God, to help her. Then she said:

WHAT OF THE RESULT?

"I looked down at her in her misery, and thought, There is a soul for whom Christ died, and if she had been the only lost one in the world he would have suffered and died for her. Then I forgot her sin and saw her soul. I forgot her misery, and my heart was filled with love for her. I stooped, and taking her sin-stained face in both my hands, I kissed her first upon one cheek, then upon the other, and that broke her heart; she fell sobbing before me. We put her in bed, nursed her back to a semblance of strength, and then she went forth, herself a missionary, down into the Mulberry Street dives, out into Sing Sing prison, everywhere where she felt that she might win a soul for Christ. She went by day and night. After a few months of active service God called her to himself, but she had been instrumental in leading over one hundred girls like herself into the knowledge of a Saviour." I asked my friend, Mr. Hadley, Jerry McAuley's successor in the old Water Street Mission: "Mr. Hadley, how did Blue Bird look: was she beautiful?" His reply was: "If you had seen her face in repose you might have said that she was homely, for her face still bore the marks of her sin; but," said he, "if you had seen her in the Water Street Mission, and heard her tell the story of her conversion, and then seen her stand with face uplifted, as if she were looking into the very face of Him who had made her free, and heard her as she repeated his name over and over—'JESUS! JESUS! JÈSUS!'— you would have said, I am sure, that she

WHAT OF THE RESULT?

looked like an angel." Then I asked him, "What was the secret of her power?" He gave me two reasons. "First of all," he said, "she was fully saved; then after that" he said, "she was filled with the Spirit. Blue Bird had never a thought of her own; she belonged to him body, soul, and spirit." And when he told me that, I said: "Blessed God, if thou canst take a poor fallen girl and so fill her with thy Spirit that she could be transformed into a soul-winner, thou canst fill me;" and I believe he can—nay, more, I believe he did; and what he has done for one he can do for all, for, as has been said, he is no respecter of persons.

But there are certain particular results which would be manifest in the life of every one who would give the Spirit undisputed possession of his life.

First. We should know God better: " For what man knoweth the things of a man, save the spirit of man which is in him? even so the things of God knoweth no man, but the Spirit of God. Now we have received, not the spirit of the world, but the Spirit which is of God; that we might know the things that are freely given to us of God. Which things also we speak, not in the words which man's wisdom teacheth, but which the Holy Ghost teacheth; comparing spiritual things with spiritual. But the natural man receivth not the things of the Spirit of God: for they are foolishness unto him: neither can he know them, because they are spiritually discerned." (1 Cor. ii. 11–14.)

Second. We should be better able to apprehend Christ, for you will remem-

WHAT OF THE RESULT?

ber that the Spirit came into the world to testify of him. There is a hint of this in the very course of the river which ran from the sanctuary. There would have been no point at all if any other direction had been given as the course of the river, but the east is most significant. The camp of Israel was always pitched toward the east—the sunrising—because Israel was looking and longing for the coming of the Messiah. The east is connected with the resurrection and with the coming glory of Christ. What can the course of the river signify but the fact that the Spirit always runs, if we may so speak of him, toward Christ? —to know one is to know the other. Do you not remember that when Jesus breathed on the disciples and said, " Receive ye the Holy Ghost," it was after

His resurrection? Was he not then, in the gift of the Spirit, just giving them the first taste of "resurrection life" for themselves? And this is, in fact, what the indwelling of the Spirit may mean for every one. We are "risen with Christ," and the Spirit just reveals to us what that means. And yet, with all the joy that is imparted here in this present time, this is but the earnest of what is coming by and by. He is called the Earnest, as, for example: "Now he which stablisheth us with you in Christ, and hath anointed us, is God; who hath also sealed us, and given the earnest of the Spirit in our hearts." (2 Cor. i. 21, 22.) An earnest is often represented as a pledge, but this does not give the real idea. It is rather part of the purchase-money, paid down

WHAT OF THE RESULT?

as the guaranty and security that the full amount will be handed over at the time stipulated in the contract. The meaning, then, is simply this: all that the indwelling Spirit may have meant to you in the past in the way of sweetness of experience, depth of joy, delight in communion, or manifestation of power —these things are just the foretaste of what is coming after a while. When the fullness of time is come, if this is the first-fruit, then what must the harvest be? Here we have thought about him, he has come to us in the night visions, we have said over and over his dear name, but then we shall see him and we shall be like him.

> "Well, the delightful day will come
> When my dear Lord will bring me home,
> And I shall see his face.

> Then with my Saviour, Brother, Friend,
> A blest eternity I'll spend,
> > Triumphant in his grace."

Third. There will be growth. This would naturally follow because of what we have found the Spirit to be. He is the wind, the dew, the rain, and many other things, all of which induce growth in the natural world. There will be a growth downward: "Rooted and built up in him" (Col. ii. 7); growth upward: "Into him in all things, which is the head, even Christ" (Eph. iv. 15); growth outward in all the fruit of the Spirit. I am sure that, with this thought of growth in mind, many of the troublesome questions in the life of the church might be settled. Paul had this in mind when he said, "When I was a child, I spake as a child, I understood as a child,

WHAT OF THE RESULT?

I thought as a child: but when I became a man, I put away childish things." (1 Cor. xiii. 11.)

Try the question of the so-called popular amusements of the day with this idea of growth in mind. See how quickly it could be settled. It is not to be denied that there is a certain kind of pleasure in some of the things which are manifestly inconsistent in the lives of professing Christians. But it is just as true that the real Christian has in his life that which is far beyond the mere pleasure of the world —that they are not comparable: but there must be growth to appreciate this. You remember the island of which we read in mythology—the island on which the sirens sang so sweetly that when a ship would come near its sailors would be charmed with the music. They would leave their posts of duty, and the vessel would be wrecked on the rocks. Then the sirens would put forth from the island to gather the spoil. One day a vessel neared the island having Ulysses as commander. He filled the sailors' ears with wax, and bade them fasten him to the mast, and then forbade their releasing him, whatever his commands might be under the spell of the music. When they neared the island it seemed as if the sirens had never sung so sweetly. Ulysses struggled to be free; he shouted to the sailors to let him go, but they did not hear him, and they would not let him go. They passed the island in safety. This was one way of going by. It is the way some would have us settle the question

WHAT OF THE RESULT?

of "amusements for the church." But there is a better way. Another vessel came near the island of the sirens. The officers did not order wax to be placed in the sailors' ears, neither was the commander fastened to the mast. The sirens sang their sweetest songs, they played their most entrancing music, but the sailors did not turn their heads to listen, and for this reason: they had Orpheus on board, and Orpheus sang a sweeter song than the sirens ever knew. Thanks be unto God, we may have Orpheus on board: we have a peace the world can never know! But the ear must be trained to hear the music. Just as when Jesus was on earth, at one time it was said: "Then came there a voice from heaven, saying, I have both glorified it, and will glorify it again. The people therefore that stood by, and heard it, said that it thundered: others said, An angel spake to him." (John xii. 28, 29.) I believe it was the voice of God to him—what some called thunder, and others an angel's voice. He called the voice of God to himself; they heard with their ears, he with his soul.

There is something very suggestive to me in the fact that the river increased in depth as it ran to the sea. "And when the man that had a line in his hand went forth eastward, he measured a thousand cubits." (Ezek. xlvii. 3.) At this first measurement the " waters were to the ankles." I use my ankles to walk with; I could hardly walk without them; and I believe it to be a hint, at least, of the fact that when one has been filled with the Holy Ghost

WHAT OF THE RESULT?

he will manifest the fact in his daily walk. What is it to walk in the Spirit? It is to have him so enthroned in the soul, and to live in such habitual and uninterrupted communion with him, that we do not take a step without his direction. It is to recognize his abiding presence, to heed his slightest suggestion, to be lifted into a purer and sweeter atmosphere than that which surrounds the world. The second measurement, and the "waters were to the knees." I bow the knees to pray. No one really knows how to pray until he knows the Spirit. How often we wonder why our prayers have not been answered! I doubt not but that the real reason could be found just here: we did not ask in the right way. "Likewise the Spirit also helpeth our infirmities: for we know not what we should pray for as we ought: but the Spirit himself maketh intercession for us with groanings which cannot be uttered." (Rom. viii. 26.) The third measurement, and the "waters were to the loins." The loins are always in the Scripture the symbol of strength, and what can this suggest but that the Spirit is the strength of our life? With him temptation is easily met, burden-bearing becomes a delight, and we can do all things just because he fills us. "Afterward he measured a thousand; and it was a river that I could not pass over: for the waters were risen, waters to swim in, a river that could not be passed over." (Ezek. xlvii. 5.) There is one thing about swimming which every swimmer knows, namely, this: when he swims he brings into play

WHAT OF THE RESULT?

every muscle of his body—not one is inactive. Thanks be unto God, the Spirit may sway every power of my being: the heart purified, the mind quickened, the soul uplifted! He gives me a new name, a new song, a new hope—in fact, "old things are passed away;" the very world itself becomes new.

But one of the very best things we read about the river is this: "And by the river upon the bank thereof, on this side and on that side, shall grow all trees for meat, whose leaf shall not fade, neither shall the fruit thereof be consumed: it shall bring forth new fruit according to his months, because their waters they issued out of the sanctuary: and the fruit thereof shall be for meat, and the leaf thereof for medicine." (Ezek. xlvii. 12.) There was new fruit every month—what a river it must have been! I do not know anything better about the Spirit than this: he brings not only things old, but things new, before us. We shall not need to live on old manna if we have him. We shall not need to be rehearsing old experiences told a thousand times if we know him; but the world will be a new world, the Bible a new book, all things will wear a different face to us, if we be "filled with the Spirit." I know of no better illustration to make plain what his indwelling may mean than that which has been given us in the life and death of one of earth's noble women. Over in London, some time ago, a noble woman died. God touched her eyes, and they were closed; her heart, and it ceased its beating. They carried her into one of

WHAT OF THE RESULT?

the greatest auditoriums, that the city and the world might pay her honor. A representative of the Queen honored herself by being present. Lords and ladies were there; the rich people of England came to look and weep. At last the poor people came pressing their way into the great building. The weeping thousands passed beside the sleeping woman. At last a very poor woman made her way down the aisle. She had every mark of poverty; she carried a child on one arm, and led another by the hand. When she reached the coffin she put the baby on the floor, loosed the clasp of the older child's hand, and then stooped to kiss the glass which covered the face. She thereby stopped the passing of the throng. The guard, stepping forward, took her by the shoulder, saying as he did so: "Woman, you will have to move on; you are stopping the people." She lifted her face to his for a moment, and then, turning to the surging mass of people in the building, she cried out: "My friends, I will not move on! I have walked sixty miles, and carried my baby, that I might look upon this woman's face. She saved my boys from hell, and I have a right to look and to weep." Then bending down she kissed again and again the glass covering the face, while the multitude sobbed in sympathy with her. Who was she sleeping in the coffin yonder? Why, that was Mrs. Booth, the mother of the Salvation Army, one of the grandest women God has ever called into his service, and I am sure you know why: not because her social position was better

WHAT OF THE RESULT?

than yours, for that might not be true; not because her intellectual qualifications were superior to yours, for that might be untrue; but because she was filled with the Holy Ghost. That is always the secret of POWER.

THE
BAPTISM WITH THE HOLY SPIRIT

By R. A. TORREY, D.D.

LATEST ISSUES

The Person and Work of the Holy Spirit. As Revealed in the Scriptures and in Personal Experience. Cloth, net $1.00.

Difficulties and Alleged Errors and Contradictions in the Bible. 12mo, Cloth, net 50c.; Paper, 15c.

Practical and Perplexing Questions Answered. 12mo, Cloth, net 50.

Anecdotes and Illustrations. Illustrated, 12mo, Cloth, net 75c.; Paper, net 35c.

FOR REVIVAL WORK

How to Bring Men to Christ. Cloth, 75c.; Paper, net 25c.

How to Work for Christ. 8vo, Cloth, $2.50.

How to Promote and Conduct a Successful Revival. New Edition, net $1.00.

REVIVAL TALKS AND ADDRESSES

The Bible and Its Christ. Cloth, net 75c.; Paper, net 25c.

Revival Addresses. Clo., net $1., pa., net 50.

Real Salvation and Whole-Hearted Service. 12mo, Cloth, net $1.00., paper, net 50.

FOR BIBLE STUDY

What the Bible Teaches. 8vo, Cloth, $2.50.

The Divine Origin of the Bible. 12mo, Cloth, 50c.

How to Study the Bible for Greatest Profit. 12mo, Cloth, 75c.

FOR THE CHRISTIAN LIFE

How to Succeed in the Christian Life. Cloth net 50c.; Paper, net 25c.

How to Pray. 12mo, Cloth, 50c.; Paper, 15c

How to Obtain Fullness of Power in Christian Life and Service. Cloth, 50c.

The Baptism With the Holy Spirit. 12mo, Cloth, 50c.

A Vest Pocket Companion for Christian Workers. Leatherette, net 25c.

THE
BAPTISM WITH THE HOLY SPIRIT

BY

R. A. TORREY

Author of " How to Bring Men to Christ," " Vest Pocket Companion," etc., etc.

"*Wait for the promise of the Father.*"—*Acts 1: 4.*
"*Ye shall be baptized with the Holy Spirit not many days hence.*"—*Acts 1: 5.*
"*Ye shall receive power after that the Holy Ghost is come upon you.*"—*Acts 1: 8.*
"*For to you is the promise, and to your children, and to all that are afar off, even as many as the Lord our God shall call unto Him.*"—*Acts 11: 39, R. V.*

NEW YORK   CHICAGO   TORONTO
Fleming H. Revell Company
LONDON AND EDINBURGH

Copyrighted 1895 and 1897, by Fleming H. Revell Company.

CONTENTS

Introduction 7

Chapter I. The Baptism with the Holy Spirit: what it is and what it does 9

Chapter II. The Necessity and Possibility of the Baptism with the Holy Spirit 25

Chapter III. How the Baptism with the Holy Spirit can be Obtained. 37

Chapter IV. "Fresh Baptisms with the Holy Spirit," or the Refilling with the Holy Spirit . . 63

Chapter V. How Spiritual Power is Lost 66

INTRODUCTION

It was a great turning point in my ministry, when, after much thought and study and meditation, I became satisfied that the Baptism with the Holy Spirit was an experience for to-day and for me, and set myself about obtaining it. Such blessing came to me personally, that I began giving Bible readings on the subject, and with increasing frequency as the years have passed. God in His wondrous grace has so greatly blessed these readings, and so many have asked for them in printed form, convenient for circulation among their friends, that I have decided to write them out in full for publication. It is an occasion of great joy that so many and such excellent books on the person and work of the Holy Spirit have appeared of late. I wish to call especial attention to two of these: "Through the Eternal Spirit," by James Elder Cumming and "The Spirit of Christ," by Andrew Murray.

In the following pages I speak uniformly of the Holy Spirit, but in the quotations from the Bible retain the less desirable phraseology there used—" The Holy Ghost "—except in those instances where the translators themselves varied their usage. Probably most of the readers of this book already know that "the Holy Spirit" and "the Holy Ghost" are simply two different translations of precisely the same Greek words. It seems very unfortunate, and almost unaccountable, that the English revisers did not follow the suggestion of the American Committee, and, for "Holy Ghost", adopt uniformly the rendering "Holy Spirit."

THE BAPTISM WITH THE HOLY SPIRIT

CHAPTER I

THE BAPTISM WITH THE HOLY SPIRIT: WHAT IT IS AND WHAT IT DOES

While a great deal is said in these days concerning the Baptism with the Holy Spirit, it is to be feared that there are many who talk about it and pray for it, who have no clear and definite idea of what it is. But the Bible, if carefully studied, will give us a view of this wondrous blessing that is perfectly clear and remarkably definite.

1. We find first of all, that *there are a number of designations in the Bible for this one experience.* In Acts 1: 5, Jesus said, "*Ye shall be baptized with the Holy Ghost not many days hence.*" In Acts 2: 4, when this promise was fulfilled, we read, "*they were all filled with the Holy Ghost.*" In Acts 1: 4, the same experience is spoken of as "*the promise of the*

Father" and in Luke 24: 49 as *" the promise of my Father,"* and *" endued power from on high."* By a comparison of Acts 10: 44, 45, 47 with Acts 11: 15, 16, we find that the expressions *" the Holy Spirit fell on them "* and *" the gift of the Holy Ghost,"* and *" received the Holy Ghost "* are all equivalent to *" baptized with the Holy Ghost."*

2. We find in the next place, that *the Baptism with the Holy Spirit is a definite experience of which one may know whether he has received it or not.* This is evident from our Savior's command to the Apostles: "Tarry ye in the city, until ye be endued with power from on high." (Luke 24: 49.) Unless this enduement with power, or Baptism with the Holy Ghost, is an experience so definite that one can know whether he has received it or not, how could they tell when those commanded days of tarrying were at an end? The same thing is clear from Paul's very definite question to the disciples at Ephesus. "Did ye receive the Holy Ghost when ye believed?" (Acts 19: 2, R. V.) Paul evidently expected a definite "yes," or a definite "no" for an answer. Unless the experience is definite, and of such a character that one can know whether he has received it or not, how could these disciples answer Paul's

question? In point of fact, they knew they had not "received," or been "baptized with," the Holy Ghost, and a short time afterward they knew they had "received," or been "baptized with," the Holy Ghost. (Acts 19: 6.) Ask many a man to-day, who prays that he may be baptized with the Holy Ghost: "Well, my brother, did you get what you asked? Were you baptized with the Holy Ghost?" and he would qe dumb-founded. He did not expect anything so definite that he could answer positively to a question like that, "yes" or "no." But we find in the Bible none of that vagueness and indefiniteness regarding this subject which we find in much of our modern prayer and speech. The Bible is a very definite book. It is very definite about salvation: so definite that a man who knows his Bible can say positively "yes" or "no" to the question "are you saved." It is equally definite about "the Baptism with the Holy Ghost:" so definite that a man who knows his Bible can say positively, "yes," or "no," to the question, "have you been baptized with the Holy Ghost." There may be those who are saved who do not know it, because they do not understand their Bibles, but it is their privilege to know it. So there may be those who have been Baptized with the Holy Ghost, who do not know the Bible name for what has come to them, but it is their privilege to know.

3. *The Baptism with the Holy Spirit is a work of the Holy Spirit separate and distinct from His regenerating work.* To be regenerated by the Holy Spirit is one thing, to be baptized with the Holy Spirit is something different, something additional. This is evident from Acts 1:5. There Jesus said: "Ye shall be baptized with the Holy Ghost *not many days hence.*" They where not then as yet "baptized with the Holy Ghost." But they were *already* regenerated. Jesus Himself had already pronounced them so. In John 15:3, He had said to the same men, "Now are ye clean through the Word." (Comp. Jas. 1:18; 1 Pet. 1:23) and in Jno. 13:10: "Ye are clean, but not all," excepting, by the "but not all," the one unregenerate man in the Apostolic company, Judas Iscariot, from the statement "Ye are clean." (See Jno. 13:11.) The Apostles, excepting Judas Iscariot, were then already regenerate men, but they were not yet "baptized with the Holy Ghost." From this it is evident that regeneration is one thing, and that the baptism with the Holy Spirit is something different, something additional. One may be regenerated and still not yet be baptized with the Holy Ghost. The

same thing is evident from Acts 8: 12-16. Here we find a company of believers who had been baptized. Surely in this company of baptized believers there were some regenerate men. But the record informs us that when Peter and John came down they "prayed for them that they might receive the Holy Ghost: (for *as yet He was fallen upon none of them*)." It is clear then that one may be a believer, may be a regenerate man, and yet not have the Baptism with the Holy Spirit. In other words, the Baptism with the Holy Spirit is something distinct from and beyond His regenerating work. Not every regenerate man has the Baptism with the Holy Spirit, though as we shall see later, every regenerate man may have this Baptism. If a man has experienced the regenerating work of the Holy Spirit he is a saved man, but he is not fitted for service until in addition to this he has received the Baptism with the Holy Spirit.

But while the baptism with the Spirit is an operation of the Holy Spirit separate and distinct from His regenerating work it may and often does occur simultaneously with it. A man may be baptized with the Spirit the moment he is regenerated. It was so in the case of the household of Cornelius. It is so in the case of many to-day. It would be so in every case in a perfectly normal condition of the Church. The apostles expected that when men were converted and regenerated they should also be baptized with the Holy Spirit at once and fitted for immediate service. (Eph. 1:13; R. V. Acts 3:38, 1 Cor. 12:13; Acts 8:15, 16; 9:17; 19:2: R. V.) In some cases, as at Ephesus, (Acts19:1-6) and Samaria, (Acts 8:12-16), because of inadequate instruction, or other reasons, this was not the case. The Ephesus or Samaria condition of affairs seems to be the prevailing condition to= day and we need to go about asking as Paul did at Ephesus " Have ye received the Holy Ghost since ye believed" (Acts 19: 2.), and insisting that regeneration is not enough but, that believers must also be baptized with the Holy Spirit.

4. *The baptism with the Holy Spirit is always connected with testimony and service.* Look carefully at every passage in which the Baptism with the Holy Spirit is mentioned, and you will see that it is connected with, and is for the purpose of, testimony and service. (For example, Acts 1:5, 8; 2:4; 4:31, 33.) This will come out very clearly when we come to consider what the Baptism with the Holy Spirit does. The Baptism with the Holy Spirit, is not an experience that God grants to us merely to make us happy. It will indeed bring into our lives a joy such as we never knew before. But that is

not its main purpose. The Baptism with the Spirit is not intended to make us happy but to make us effective. We should not look and long for ecstatic experiences, but for power and efficiency for God. The Baptism with the Holy Spirit is not even primarily for the purpose of cleansing from sin, but for the purpose of empowering for service. There is a line of teaching, put forward by a very earnest but mistaken body of people, that has brought the whole doctrine of the Baptism with the Holy Spirit into disrepute. It runs this way: First proposition: there is a further experience (or second blessing) after regeneration, namely, the Baptism with the Holy Spirit. This proposition is true and can be easily proven from the Bible. Second proposition: this Baptism with the Holy Spirit can be instantaneously received. This proposition is also true and can be easily proven from the Bible. Third proposition: this Baptism with the Holy Spirit is the eradication of the sinful nature. This proposition is untrue. Not a line of Scripture can be adduced to show that the Baptism with the Holy Spirit is the eradication of the sinful nature. The conclusion, viz., "the sinful nature can be instantaneously eradicated," drawn from these three propositions, two true and one false, is necessarily false. The the purpose of cleansing from sin, but for the

Baptism with the Holy Spirit is not primarily for purpose of empowering for service. It is indeed the work of the Holy Spirit to cleanse from sin. Further than this there is a work of the Holy Spirit where the believer is strengthened with might in the inner man: that Christ may dwell in his heart by faith . . . that he might be filled unto all the fulness of God. (Eph. 3: 16–19 R. V.) There is a work of the Holy Spirit of such a character that the believer is "made free from the law of sin and death," (Rom. 8: 2) and through the Spirit does "mortify (put to death) the deeds of the body." (Rom. 8:13.) It is our privilege to so walk, daily and hourly, in the power of the Spirit, that the carnal nature is kept in the place of death. But this is not the Baptism with the Spirit, neither is it the *eradication* of the sinful nature. It is not something done once for all, it is something that must be momentarily maintained. "*Walk* in the Spirit, and ye shall not fulfil the lust of the flesh." (Gal. 5:16.)

While insisting that the Baptism with the Spirit is primarily, for the purpose of empowering for service, it should beadded that the Baptism is accompanied by a great moral uplift. It ought to mean and usually does means a transformed life as well as a transformed ministry.

(See Acts 2: 44–46; 4: 31–35.) This is necessarily so, from the steps one must take to obtain this blessing. Further than this we cannot forget that one of the promises on this subject reads: " He shall baptize you with the Holy Ghost, *and with fire.*" (Matt. 3:11.) When we notice that here fire seems to be contrasted with water in the earlier part of the verse, it is hard to avoid the conclusion that the cleansing power of fire is partly in mind. If this be so, then the Baptism with the Holy Spirit which is *primarily* an energizing process, is also a revealing, refining, consuming, illuminating process, and one by which we are made to glow with love to God, and love to man, and love to souls.

5. We will get a still clearer and fuller view of what the Baptism with the Holy Spirit is, if we will notice what this Baptism does. This is stated concisely in Acts 1: 8. " Ye shall receive *power* after that the Holy Ghost is come upon you; and ye shall be witnesses," etc. The Baptism with the Holy Spirit imparts *"power"* power for service. This power will not manifest itself in precisely the same way in each individual. This is brought out very clearly in 1 Cor. 12:4–13, R.V.: "Now there are diversities of gifts but the same spirit. For to one is given, through the Spirit, the word of wisdom; and to

another the word of knowledge, according to the same spirit; to another faith, in the same spirit; and to another gifts of healing, in the one spirit; to another diverse kinds of tongues; but all these worketh the one and the same spirit, dividing to each one severally even as He will." In my early study of the Baptism with the Holy Spirit, I noticed that in many instances those who were so baptized "spoke with tongues," and the question came often into my mind: if one is baptized with the Holy Spirit will he not speak with tongues? But I saw no one so speaking, and I often wondered, is there any one to-day who actually is baptized with the Holy Spirit. This twelfth chapter of 1st Corinthians cleared me up on that, especially when I found Paul asking of those who had been baptized with the Holy Spirit: "Do all speak with tongues?" (1 Cor. 12: 30.) But I fell into another error, namely, that any one who received the Baptism with the Holy Spirit would receive power as an evangelist, or as a preacher of the Word. This is equally contrary to the teaching of the chapter, that "there are *diversities of gifts*, but the one Spirit." There are three evils arising from the mistake just mentioned. First, disappointment. Many will seek the Baptism with the Holy Spirit, expecting power as an evangelist, but

God has not called them to that work, and the power that comes from the Baptism with the Holy Spirit manifests itself in another way in them. Many cases of bitter disappointment and almost despair have arisen from this cause. The second evil is graver than the first: presumption. A man whom God has not called to the work of an evangelist, or minister, rushes into it because he has received, or thinks he has received, the Baptism with the Holy Spirit. Many a man has said: "All a man needs to succeed as a preacher is the Baptism with the Holy Spirit." This is not true. He needs a call to that specific work, and he needs the study of the Word of God that will prepare him for the work. The third evil is still greater: indifference. There are many who know they are not called to the work of preaching. For example, a mother with a large family of children knows this. If then, they think that the Baptism with the Holy Spirit simply imparts power to preach, it is a matter of no personal concern to them; but when we come to see the truth that, while the Baptism with the Spirit imparts power, the way in which that power will be manifested, depends upon the work to which God has called us, and that no efficient work can be done without it, then the mother will see that she equally with the preacher needs this Baptism—needs it for that most important and hallowed of all work, to bring up her children "in the nurture and admonition of the Lord." I have recently met a very happy mother. A few months ago she heard of the Baptism with the Holy Spirit, sought it and received it. "Oh," she joyfully exclaimed as she told me the story, "Since I received it, I have been able to get into the hearts of my children which I was never able to do before."

It is the Holy Spirit Himself who decides how the power will manifest itself in any given case: "the spirit dividing to each one severally even as *He* will." (1 Cor. 12:11 R. V.) We have a right "to desire earnestly the greater gifts" (1 Cor. 12;31.), but the Holy Spirit is sovereign, and He not we, must determine in the final issue. It is not for us then to select some gift, and then look to the Holy Spirit to impart the self-chosen gift; it is not for us to select some field of service and then look to the Holy Spirit to impart to us power in that field which we, and not He, have chosen. It is rather for us to recognize the Divinity and sovereignty of the Spirit, and put ourselves unreservedly at His disposal; for Him to select the gift that "He will" and impart to us that gift; for Him to select for us the field that "He will" and impart to us the power that will qualify us for the field He has chosen. I once knew a child of God, who, hearing of the Baptism with the Holy Spirit and the power that resulted from it, gave up at a great sacrifice, the secular work in which he was engaged, and entered upon the work of an evangelist. But the expected power in that line did not follow. The man fell into great doubt and darkness, until he was led to see that the Holy Spirit divideth "to each one severally, even as He will." Then giving up selecting his own field and gifts, he put himself at the Holy Spirit's disposal for Him to choose. In the final outcome the Holy Spirit did impart to this man power as an evangelist and a preacher of the Word. We must then surrender ourselves absolutely to the Holy Spirit to work as He will.

But, while the power that the Baptism with the Holy Spirit brings, manifests itself in different ways in different individuals, there will always be power. Just as surely as a man is baptized with the Holy Spirit there will be new power, a power not his own, "the power of the Highest!" Religious biography abounds in instances of men, who have worked along as best they could, until one day they were led to see there was such an experience as the Baptism with the Holy Spirit, and to seek it and obtain it. From that hour there came into their service a new power that utterly transformed its character. Finney, Brainerd and Moody are a few of the many cases in point. Cases of this character are not confined to a few exceptional men, they are becoming common. The writer has personally met and corresponded with hundreds during the past twelve months, who could testify definitely to the new power that God had granted them through the Baptism with the Holy Spirit. These hundreds of men and women were in all branches of Christian service. Many of them were ministers of the gospel, others mission workers, others Y. M. C. A. secretaries, others Sunday=school teachers, others personal workers, others fathers and mothers. Nothing could exceed the clearness, confidence and joyfulness of many of these testimonies. What we have in promise in the words of Christ many have, and all may have, in glad experience: "Ye shall receive power, after that the Holy Ghost is come upon you."

6. There is another but closely related result of the Baptism with the Holy Spirit in Acts 4: 31. "They were all filled with the Holy Ghost, and they spake the Word of God *with*

boldness." The Baptism with the Holy Spirit imparts to those who receive it new liberty and fearlessness in testimony for Christ. The same Peter, who before his baptism with the Holy Spirit, cowered at the maid's charge that he was one of Jesus' disciples (Jno. 18: 17) after his baptism with the Holy Spirit, faces the very council that put Jesus to death and says: "The God of our fathers raised up Jesus whom ye slew and hanged upon a tree." (Acts 5: 30) The natural timidity and constraint of many a man to-day, vanishes when he is filled with the Holy Spirit, and with great boldness and liberty and fearlessness he gives his testimony for Christ.

7. The Baptism with the Holy Spirit causes the one who receives it to be occupied with God and Christ and spiritual things. On the day of Pentecost it was "the mighty works of God," (Acts 2: 11) of which the Spirit-filled men and women spoke. Peter's sermon on that day is all about Christ, and especially about His resurrection. (Acts 2: 22–36, compare also Acts 4: 8–10, 31, 33). When Saul of Tarsus had been filled with the Holy Spirit, "straightway in the synagogues he *proclaimed Jesus.*" (Acts 9: 17, 20). When Cornelius and his household were baptised with the Holy Spirit they began at once

to "magnify God" (Acts 10: 44–46). Men who are baptized with the Holy Ghost do not talk much about self, but very much of God, and especially about Christ. This is naturally so, as it is the Spirit's office to "bear witness of" and "glorify" Christ. (Jno. 15: 26, R. V. 16: 14.) Paul says that the result of being "filled with the Holy Spirit" is that men speak "to one another in psalms and hymns and spiritual songs, singing and making melody with their hearts to the Lord." (Eph. 5: 18, 19.) Worldly songs loose their charm to one who is baptized with the Holy Spirit; he is occupied with Christ.

To sum up the contents of this chapter: The Baptism with the Holy Spirit is the Spirit of God coming upon the believer, taking possession of his faculties, imparting to him gifts not naturally his own, but which qualify him for the service to which God has called him.

CHAPTER II

THE NECESSITY AND POSSIBILITY OF THE BAPTISM WITH THE HOLY SPIRIT

Shortly before Christ was received up into heaven, having committed the preaching of the gospel to His disciples, He laid upon them this very solemn charge concerning the beginning of the great work He had committed to their hands: "Behold, I send forth the promise of my Father upon you; but tarry ye in the city, until ye be clothed with power from on high." (Luke 24: 49, R. V.) There is no doubt as to what Jesus meant by the "promise of my Father" for which they were to wait before beginning the ministry which He had intrusted to them; for in Acts 1: 4, 5, we read that Jesus "charged them not to depart from Jerusalem, but to wait for *the promise of the Father*" which, said he, "Ye heard from me: for John indeed baptized with water: but ye shall be *baptized with the Holy Ghost* not many days hence." "The promise of the Father," through which the enduement of power was to come, was the Baptism with the Holy

Spirit. (Comp. Acts 1: 8). Christ then strictly charged His disciples not to presume to undertake the work to which He had called them until they had received as the necessary and all-essential preparation for that work, the Baptism with the Holy Spirit. The men to whom Jesus said this, seemed to have already received very thorough preparation for the work in hand. They had been to school to Christ Himself for more than three years. They had heard from His own lips the great truths that they were to proclaim to the world. They had been eye-witnesses of His miracles, of His death and of His resurrection and were about to be eye-witnesses of His ascension. The work before them was simply to go forth to proclaim what their own eyes had seen and what their own ears had heard from the lips of Christ Himself. Were they not fully prepared for this work? It would seem so to us. But Christ said: "No. You are so utterly unprepared you must not stir a step yet. There is a further preparation, so all-essential to effective service, that you must abide at Jerusalem until you receive it. This further preparation is the Baptism with the Holy Spirit. When you receive that— and *not until then*—you will be prepared to begin the work to which I have called you." If Christ did not permit these men, who had received so rare and unparalleled a schooling for the work to which He had so definitely and clearly called them, to undertake this without receiving in addition to that the Baptism with the Holy Spirit, what is it for us to undertake the work to which He has called us until we have received, in addition to any amount of schooling we may have had for the work, the Baptism with the Holy Spirit? Is it not most daring presumption?

But this is not all. In Acts 10: 38, we read "how God anointed Jesus of Nazareth with the Holy Ghost and with power: who went about doing good, and healing all that were oppressed of the devil." When we look into the gospels for an explanation of these words, we find it in Luke 3: 21, 22; 4: 1, 14, 15, 18, 21. We find that at the Baptism of Jesus at Jordan *as He prayed*, the Holy Spirit came upon Him. Then, "*full* of the Holy Ghost," He has the temptation experience. Then, "*in the power of Spirit*," He begins His ministry, and proclaims himself "*anointed* to preach" because "*the Spirit of the Lord is upon* Him." In other words, Jesus the Christ, never entered upon the ministry for which He came into this world until He was baptized with the Holy Spirit. If Jesus Christ, who had been supernaturally conceived through the Holy Spirit's power, who was the only begotten Son of God, who was divine, very God of very God, and yet truly man; if such an one, "leaving us an example that we should follow in His steps," did not venture upon the ministry for which the Father had sent Him until thus baptised with the Holy Ghost, what is it for us to dare to do it? If, in the light of these recorded facts, we dare to do it, it seems like an offence going beyond presumption. Doubtless it has been done in ignorance by many, but can we plead ignorance any longer? *The Baptism with the Holy Spirit is an absolutely necessary preparation for effective service for Christ along every line of service.* We may have a very clear call to service, as clear it may be as the Apostles had, but the charge is laid upon us, as upon them, that before we begin that service we must "tarry until ye be clothed with power from on high." This enduement with power is through the Baptism with the Holy Spirit. There are certainly few greater mistakes that we are making to-day, than that of setting men to teach Sunday-school classes, and do personal work, and even to preach the gospel, simply because they have been converted and received a certain amount of education—perhaps including a college and seminary course—but have not as yet been baptized with the Holy Spirit. Any man who is in Christian work, who has not received the Baptism with the Holy Spirit, ought to stop his work right where he is, and not go on with it until he has been "clothed with power from on high." But what will our work do while we are waiting? What did the world do those ten days while the early disciples were waiting? They alone knew the saving truth, yet, in obedience to the Lord's command, they were silent. The world was no loser. When the power came they accomplished more in one day than they would have accomplished in years, if they had gone on in presumptuous disobedience to Christ's charge; so will we after we have received the Baptism with the Holy Spirit accomplish more in one day than we ever would in years without His power. Days spent in waiting, if it were necessary, would be well spent, but we shall see further on that there is no need that we spend days in waiting. It may be said that the Apostles had gone out on missionary tours during Christ's lifetime before they were baptized with the Holy Spirit. This is true, but that was before the Holy Ghost was given, and before the charge, "tarry until ye be clothed with power from on high" was given. After that it would have been disobedience and presumption to have gone forth without this enduement, and we are living to-day after the Holy Ghost has been given and after the charge to "tarry until clothed" has been given.

We come now to the question of the Possibility of the Baptism with the Holy Spirit. Is the Baptism with the Holy Spirit for us? This is a question that has a most plain and explicit answer in the Word of God. In Acts 2: 39, R. V., we read: "For to you is the promise, and to your children and to all that are afar off, *even as many as the Lord our God shall call unto Him.*" What is "the promise" of this passage? Turning back to the fourth and fifth verses of the preceding chapter we read: "Wait for *the promise* of the Father, which, saith He, ye have heard of Me. For John truly baptised with water; but *ye shall be baptized with the Holy Ghost* not many days hence." Again in the thirty-third verse of the second chapter we read: "Having received of the Father *the promise of the Holy Ghost.*" It would seem to be perfectly clear that "the promise" of the thirty-ninth verse must be the same as "the promise" of the thirty-third verse and "the promise" of the fourth and fifth verses of the preceding chapter; *i. e.*, the prom-

NECESSITY OF THE BAPTISM 31

ise of the Baptism with the Holy Spirit. This conclusion is rendered absolutely certain by the context: "Repent and be baptized every one of you in the name of Jesus Christ unto the remission of your sins, and *ye shall receive the gift of the Holy Ghost.* For to you is the promise," etc. The promise then of this verse is the promise of the gift or Baptism with the Holy Ghost. (Comp. Acts 10:45 with Acts 11: 15, 16, to prove that "the gift of the Holy Ghost" is the same as "the Baptism with the Holy Ghost.") Who is this gift for? "To you," says Peter to the Jews whom he was immediately addressing. Then looking over their heads to the next generation, "And to your children." Then looking down all the coming ages of the Church's history to Gentile as well as Jew: "And to all that are afar off, even as many as the Lord our God shall call unto Him." The Baptism with the Holy Spirit is for every child of God in every age of the Church's history. If it is not ours in experimental possession, it is because we have not taken (the exact force of the word translated "receive" in verse 38 is *take*) what God has provided for us in our exalted Savior. (Acts 2:33; Jno. 7:38, 39.) A minister of the gospel once came to me after a lecture on the Baptism with the Holy Spirit, and said: "The church to which I belong, teaches that the Baptism with the Holy Spirit was for the Apostolic age alone." "It matters not," was replied, "what the church to which you belong, or the church to which I belong, teaches. What says the Word of God?" Acts 2:39 was read: "To you is the promise, and to your children, and to all that are afar off, even as many as the Lord our God shall call unto Him." "Has He called you?" I asked. "Yes He certainly has." "Is the promise for you?" "Yes, it is." And it was. And it is for every child of God who reads these pages. What a thrilling thought it is that the Baptism with the Holy Spirit, the enduement with *power from on high* is for us, is FOR ME individually! But that unspeakably joyous thought has its solemn side. If I may be baptized with the Holy Spirit I *must* be. If I am baptised with the Holy Spirit, then will souls be saved *through my instrumentality* who are not so saved if I am not so baptised. If then I am not willing to pay the price of this Baptism, and therefore am not so baptised, I am responsible before God for all the souls that might have been saved, but were not saved, through me, because I was not baptised with the Holy Spirit. I oftentimes tremble for my brethren in

Christian work and myself. Not because we are teaching deadly error to men; some are guilty of even that, but I do not refer to that now. Not that we are not teaching the full truth as it is in Jesus. It must be confessed that there are many, who do not teach positive error, who do not preach a full gospel, but I do not refer to that. I tremble for those who are preaching the truth, the truth as it is in Jesus, the gospel in its simplicity, in its purity, in its fulness, but preaching it "in persuasive words of wisdom" and not "in demonstration of the Spirit and of power" (1 Cor. 2: 4, R. V.), preaching it in the energy of the flesh and not in the power of the Holy Spirit. There is nothing more deadly than the gospel without the Spirit's power. "The letter killeth, but the Spirit giveth life." It is awfully solemn business preaching the gospel either from the pulpit or in more quiet ways. It means death or life to those who hear, and whether it means death or life depends very largely on whether we preach it without or with the Baptism with the Holy Spirit. We must be baptized with the Holy Spirit.

Note 1. It is sometimes argued that "the Baptism with the Holy Spirit" was for the purpose of imparting miracle-working power, and for the Apostolic age alone. In favor of this position it is asserted that the Baptism with the Holy Spirit was followed quite uniformly by miracles. The untenableness of this position is seen: (1) By the fact, that Christ Himself asserted that the purpose of the Baptism with the Holy Spirit was to impart power for witnessing—not especially power to work miracles. (Acts 1:5, 8; Luke 20: 48, 49.) (2) By the fact, that Paul distinctly taught that there were diversities of gift, and that "workings of miracles" was only one of the manifold manifestations of the Baptism with the Holy Spirit. (Cor. 12: 4, 8-10.) (3) By the fact, that Peter distinctly asserts that "the gift of the Holy Ghost," "the promise," is for all believers in all generations (Acts 2: 38, 39), and it is evident from a comparison of Acts 2: 39 with Luke 24: 49; Acts 1: 4, 5; 2: 33, and of Acts 2: 38 with Acts 10: 45 and Acts 11: 15, 16, that each of these two expressions, "the promise," and "the gift of the Holy Ghost," refers to the Baptism with the Holy Spirit. If we take miracles in the broad sense of all results wrought by supernatural power, then it is true that each one baptized with the Holy Spirit does receive miracle-working power; for each one so baptized does receive a power not naturally his own: supernatural power, God's own power. The result of the Baptism with the Holy Spirit that was most noticeable and essential was convincing, convicting and converting power. (Acts 2:4, 37, 41. Acts 4:8–13. Acts 4:31, 33. Acts 9: 17, 20–22.) There seem to have been no displays of miracle-working power immediately following Paul's Baptism with the Holy Spirit, even though he became so singularly gifted in this direction at a later day—it was power to witness for Jesus as the Son of God that he received in immediate connection with the Baptism with the Holy Spirit (Acts 9: 17, 20–22.)

Note 2. It is taught by some, that the Baptism with the Spirit is for the church as a whole and not for the individual believer, and that the whole church was baptised at Pen-

NECESSITY OF THE BAPTISM 35

tecost, and that therefore it is unwarrantable for individual believers to-day to pray or seek for a baptism with the Spirit. But the scriptures very clearly disprove this position. The record of Pentecost is that "it sat upon *each one* of them. (Acts 2: 3, R. V.) Not on the Church collectively, but upon each believer individually. This position is further shown to be untenable by the fact that the Apostles inquired of individual churches and believers whether they had received the Holy Spirit, (Acts 8: 15, 16; 19: 2,) and found, in some instances at least, that they had not, whatever the church as a whole may have received.

Note 3. An eminent Bible teacher has these strange comments to make on Acts 8: "If the Samaritan can believe and rejoice in that belief for some time without the gift of the Holy Spirit in his outward manifestations, if He cannot be so given except by the imposition of an apostle's hands, is it not plain that the time has begun when He will no longer be present in His extraordinary displays? The twelve could not go the world over to lay hands on millions." We answer, no it is not plain at all. Indeed it contradicts the plain teaching of Scripture. Acts 19: 1–6, came long after (perhaps 17 years) Acts 8: 12–16. Furthermore, though the Samaritans did "believe and rejoice in that belief for some time without the gift of the Holy Spirit," it was so important that they have it that this was the first and principal thing the apostles attended to upon their arrival. Further still the question itself contains a statement that is contrary to fact, viz: "He cannot be so given except by the imposition of an apostle's hands." In the case of Saul of Tarsus it was "a certain disciple" who imposed his hands (Acts 9: 10, 17). In the case of the household of Cornelius there was no imposition of hands at all (Acts 10: 44). It may be said "these instances are exceptional." With some people everything that does not fit a preconceived theory is exceptional. Further still this position contradicts flatly Peter's statement in Acts 2: 39. The above writer continues: "There is no hint that the Romans had this particular gift. The same is true of other churches." Let anyone who fancies this to be so read Rom. 12: 6–8; 1 Cor. 12: 7–13, 28–31; Gal. 3: 2. (Here Paul refers to a definite, conscious experience of the receiving of the Holy Spirit as a proof of God's pleasure with "the hearing of faith"); Eph. 1: 13, 14; 4: 7, 11. So far from its being evident that "the gift was not intended to be universal or permanent," it is evident that it was intended to be universal and permanent, and that men do not enter into it simply because of their unbelief. It is amazing the number of theories that have been proposed to relieve the consciences of those who are troubled at the wide gulf between their experience and the plain teaching of the Acts of the Apostles. A better way to relieve the conscience would be to find out the conditions and make one's own this blessed experience.

There is abundant present day experience confirming the teaching of the Word along these lines. While many have been trying to work out some "subtle" exegetical method of "explaining away" the seeming meaning of the Bible; others have simply believed it, and know by the indisputable proof of experience that a child of God may to-day "be baptized with the Holy Spirit," and that he does "receive power after that the Holy Ghost is come upon" him. God grant that the present reader of this book may claim this glorious "birthright" of the children of God for himself. The refining verities of believing experience immeasurably transcend the refined subtleties of unbelieving exegesis.

CHAPTER III

HOW THE BAPTISM WITH THE HOLY SPIRIT IS OBTAINED

We have now come to a place where there is a deep sense that we must be baptized with the Holy Spirit. The practical question confronts us: how can we obtain this baptism with the Holy Spirit which we so sorely need? This question also the Word of God answers very plainly and very explicitly. There is pointed out in the Bible a path, consisting of seven simple steps, which any one who will can take, and whoever takes these seven steps will, with absolute certainty, enter into this blessing. This statement may seem very positive, but the Word of God is equally positive regarding the outcome of taking these steps which it points out. All seven steps are stated or implied in Acts 2: 38: " Repent ye, and be baptized every one of you in the name of Jesus Christ unto the remission of your sins, *and ye shall receive* the gift of the Holy Ghost." The first three steps are brought out with especial definiteness and distinctness in this verse. The others, which are clearly implied in the verse, are brought out more explicitly by other passages to which we shall refer later.

1. The first two steps are found in the word "repent." What does "repent" mean? *Change your mind;* change your mind about what? About God, about Christ, about sin. As to what the change of mind is about in any given case must be determined by the context. Here the first and most prominent thought is a change of mind about Christ. Peter has just brought against his hearers the awful charge that they had crucified Him whom God had made both Lord and Christ. "Pricked in their heart" by this charge, carried home by the power of the Holy Spirit, his hearers had cried out, "Men and brethren, what shall we do?" "Repent," Peter answered. Change your mind about Christ. Change from a Christ-hating and Christ-crucifying attitude of mind to a Christ-accepting attitude of mind, Accept Jesus as Savior, Christ and Lord. *This then is the first step toward the Baptism with the Holy Spirit: Accept Jesus as Savior, Christ and Lord.* Have you taken this step? Have you accepted Jesus as your Savior? Are you relying wholly

HOW BAPTISM MAY BE OBTAINED 39

upon His atoning work for pardon? Relying solely upon the fact that He bore your sins, for acceptance before God? (1Pet. 2:24; 2 Cor. 5: 21.) There are many professed Christians who are not doing this, many who are trying to add some works of their own to the finished work of Christ, as a ground of acceptance with God. But Paul says that we receive the Spirit not "by the works of the law," but by "the hearing of faith." (Gal. 3:2.) If you have accepted Jesus as your Savior, have you also accepted Him as your Christ and Lord? That is, have you surrendered the absolute control of your life to Him? We will hear more of this further on in the fourth step.

2. The second step is also found in the word "repent." While the change of mind about Jesus is the first and prominent thought, there must also be a change of mind about sin. A change of mind from a sin-loving or sin-indulging attitude of mind to a sin-hating and sin-renouncing attitude of mind. This is the second step: *renounce sin*, all sin, every sin. Here we come upon one of the commonest obstacles to receiving the Holy Spirit—*Sin*. Something is held on to that in our inmost hearts we more or less definitely feel to be not pleasing to God. If we are to receive the Holy Spirit, there must be very honest and

very thorough heart searching. We cannot do satisfactory heart searching ourselves, God must do it. If we wish to receive the Holy Spirit, we should go alone with God and ask Him to search us thoroughly and bring to light anything that displeases Him. (Ps. 139: 23, 24.) Then we should wait for Him to do it. When the displeasing thing is revealed, it should be put away at once. If, after *patient* and *honest* waiting, nothing is brought to light, we may conclude there is nothing of this kind in the way, and proceed to the further steps. But we should not conclude this too hurriedly. It is not time lost to wait long before God as He sends the searching light of His Spirit and Word into the innermost recesses of our heart and life. It is a painful but salutary process. The sin that hinders the blessing may be something that appears very small and insignificant in itself. Mr. Finney tells of a young woman who was in deep concern regarding the Baptism with the Holy Spirit. Night after night she agonized in prayer, but the desired blessing did not come. One night as she was in prayer there came up before her some matter of head adornment that had often troubled her before; putting her hand to her head, she took the pins out and threw them away, and immediately the blessing came. This was a small matter in itself, a matter that would not have appeared to many as sin, but yet a matter of controversy between this woman and God, and when this was settled the blessing came. It may be something that you regard as very, very insignificant that is shutting you out of the Baptism with the Holy Spirit. Surely it is not insignificant if it is doing that. Whatever the controversy you have with God, have done with it. "Whatsoever is not of faith is sin" (Rom. 14: 23), and it matters not how little the thing may be, if there are questions regarding it, it must be put away, if we are to have the Baptism with the Holy Spirit. How many have agonized and prayed for the Baptism with the Holy Spirit without any result, until the obstructing sin was removed and then the blessing came. *The second step then toward the Baptism with the Holy Spirit is to put away every sin.*

3. The third step is found in this same verse: "*Be baptized in the name of Jesus Christ unto the remission of your sins.*" It was immediately after His baptism that the Holy Spirit descended upon Jesus. (Luke 3: 21, 22.) In His baptism, Jesus though Himself sinless, humbled Himself to take the sinner's place, and then God highly exalted Him

by the giving of the Holy Spirit and by the audible testimony; "Thou art my beloved son; in thee I am well pleased." So we must humble ourselves to make open confession of our sin and renunciation of it and acceptance of Jesus Christ, in God's appointed way, by baptism. The Baptism with the Holy Spirit is not for the one who secretly takes his place as a sinner and believer in Christ, but for the one who does so openly. Of course, the Baptism with the Holy Spirit may precede water baptism; as in the case, of the household of Cornelius. (Acts 10: 47.) But this was evidently an exceptional case, and water baptism immediately followed. I have little doubt that there have been those, among Christians who did not believe in or practice water baptism—as, for example, "the Friends" or "Quakers"—who have had and given evidence of the Baptism with the Holy Spirit, but the passage before us certainly presents the normal order.

4. The fourth step is clearly implied in the verse we have been studying, (Acts 2: 38) but it is brought out more explicitly in Acts 5: 32: "The Holy Ghost, whom God hath given to them that *obey Him.*" *The fourth step is obedience.* What does obedience mean? It does not mean merely doing some of the things, or many of

the things, or most of the things, that God bids us do. It means *total surrender to the will of God.* Obedience is an attitude of the will lying back of specific acts of obedience. It means that I come to God and say: " Heavenly Father, here I am and all I have. Thou hast bought me with a price and I acknowledge Thine absolute ownership. Take me and all I have, and do with me whatsoever Thou wilt. Send me where Thou wilt, use me as Thou wilt. I surrender myself and all I possess absolutely, unconditionally, forever, to Thy control and use." It was when the burnt offering, *whole*, no part held back, was laid upon the alter that "there came forth fire from before the Lord" and accepted the gift (Lev. 9: 24); and it is when we bring ourselves a *whole* burnt offering to the Lord, and lay ourselves thus upon the altar, that the fire comes and God thus accepts the gift. Here we touch upon the hindrance to the Baptism with the Holy Spirit in many lives: there is not total surrender, the will is not laid down, the heart does not cry: " Lord, where Thou wilt, what Thou wilt, as Thou wilt." One man desires the Baptism with the Holy Spirit that he may preach or work with power in Boston, when God wishes him in Bombay. Another, that he may preach to popular audiences, when

God wishes him to plod among the poor. A young woman at a convention expressed a strong desire that some one would speak on the Baptism with the Holy Spirit. The address went home with power to her heart. She had been for some time in deep travail of soul when I asked her what it was that she desired. "Oh," she cried, "I cannot go back to Baltimore until I am baptized with the Holy Spirit." "Is your will laid down?" "I don't know." "You wish to go back to Baltimore to be a Christian worker?" "Yes." "Are you willing to go back to Baltimore and be a servant girl if that is where God wishes you?" "No I am not." "Well, you will never get the Baptism with the Holy Spirit until you are. Will you lay your will down?" "I can't." "Are you willing God should lay it down for you?" "Yes." "Well, then, ask Him to do it." The head was bowed in brief but earnest prayer. "Did God hear that prayer?" "He must have, it was according to His will; He did." "Now ask Him for the Baptism with the Holy Spirit." Again the head was bowed and the brief, earnest prayer ascended to God. There was a brief silence, and the agony was over, the blessing had come—when the will was surrendered. There are many who hold back from this total surrender because they fear God's will. They are afraid God's will may be something dreadful. Remember who God is. He is our Father. Never an earthly father had so loving and tender a will regarding his children as He has toward us. "No good thing will He withhold from them that walk uprightly." (Ps. 84:11). "He that spared not His own Son, but delivered Him up for us all, how shall He not with Him also freely give us all things?" There is nothing to be feared in God's will. God's will will always prove in the final outcome the best and sweetest thing in all God's universe.

5. The fifth step is found in Jno. 7:37-39: "Jesus stood, and cried, saying, if any man *thirst*, let him come unto me, and drink. He that believeth on me, as the Scripture hath said, out of his belly shall flow rivers of living water. But this spake He of the Spirit, which they that believe on him should receive." There is also a very suggestive passage in Isaiah, the forty-fourth chapter and third verse: "I will pour water upon him that is *thirsty*. . . I will pour my Spirit upon thy seed." Matt. 5:6. is also closely related to these two passages: "Blessed are they which do hunger and *thirst* after righteousness, for they shall be filled." What does it mean to thirst? When one thirsts

there is but one cry: "Water! water! water!" Every pore in the body seems to have a voice and cry out "water." So when our hearts have one cry: "the Holy Spirit, the Holy Spirit, the Holy Spirit," then it is that God pours floods upon the dry ground, pours His Spirit upon us. *This then is the fifth step—intense desire for the Baptism with the Holy Spirit.* To what a pitch of longing the early disciples had been brought by the tenth day of their eager waiting! and their thirsty souls were filled that day when "Pentecost was fully come." As long as one thinks he can get along somehow without the Baptism with the Holy Spirit, as long as he casts about for something in the way of education, or cunningly concocted methods of work, to take its place, he is not going to receive it. There are many ministers who are missing the fulness of power God has for them, simply because they are not willing to admit the lack there has been all these years in their ministry. It is indeed a humiliating thing to confess, but that humiliating confession would be the precursor of a marvellous blessing. But there are not a few, who, in their unwillingness to make this wholesome confession, are casting about for some ingenious device of exegesis to get around the plain and simple meaning of

God's Word, and thus they are cheating themselves of that fulness of the Spirit's power which God is so eager to bestow upon them; and furthermore, they are imperilling the eternal interests of the souls that are dependent upon their ministrations, that might be won for Christ, if they had the power of the Holy Spirit which they might have. But there are others whom God in His grace brought to see that there was a something their ministry lacked, and this something nothing less than that all-essential Baptism with the Holy Spirit, without which one is utterly unqualified for acceptable and effective service. They have humbly and frankly confessed their lack. Sometimes they have been led to the God-taught resolution that they would not go on in their work until this lack was supplied. They have waited in eager longing upon God the Father for the fulfilment of His promise, and the result has been a transformed ministry for which many have risen to bless God.

It is not enough that the desire for the Baptism with the Holy Spirit be intense; it must also be pure. There is a desire for the Baptism with the Holy Spirit that is entirely selfish. Many a one has an intense desire for the Baptism with the Holy Spirit, simply that he may be a great preacher, or great personal worker, or renowned in some way as a Christian. It is simply his own gain or glory that he is seeking. After all it is not the Holy Spirit that he seeks, but his own honor, and the Baptism with the Holy Spirit simply as a means to that end. One of the subtlest and most dangerous snares into which Satan leads us, is that where we are seeking the Holy Spirit, this most solemn of all gifts, for our own ends. The desire for the Holy Spirit must not be in order to make that sublime and divine Person the servant of our low ends, but for the glory of God. It must arise from a recognition that God and Christ are being dishonored by my powerless ministry and by the sin of the people about me, against which I now have no power, and that He will be honored, if I have the Baptism with the Spirit of God. One of the most solemn passages in the New Testament bears upon this point. (Acts 8: 18–24, R. V.) "When Simon saw that through the laying on of the Apostles' hands the Holy Ghost was given, he offered them money, saying: Give me also this power, that on whomsoever I lay my hands, he may receive the Holy Ghost." Here was a strong desire on Simon's part, but it was entirely unhallowed and selfish, and Peter's terrific answer is worthy of note and meditation. Is there not many a one to-day who, with equally unhallowed and selfish purpose desires the Baptism with the Holy Spirit? Each one who is desiring and seeking the Baptism with the Holy Spirit, would do well to ask himself *why* he desires it. If you find that it is merely for your own gratification or glory, then ask God to forgive you the thought of your heart, and to enable you to see how you need it for His glory, and to desire it to that end.

6. The sixth step is shown in Luke 11: 13: "If ye then, being evil, know how to give good gifts unto your children, how much more shall your heavenly Father give the Holy Spirit to them that *ask* Him." *The sixth step is to ask.* Definite asking for a definite blessing. When Christ has been accepted as Savior and Master, and confessed as such; when sin has been put away; when there has been the definite, total surrender of the will; when there is real and holy desire; then comes the simple act of asking God for this definite blessing. It is given in answer to earnest, definite, specific, believing prayer. It has been earnestly contended by some that we should not pray for the Holy Spirit. They reason this out in this way: "The Holy Spirit was given to the Church at Pentecost as an abiding gift." This is true, and what was given

to the Church each believer must appropriate for himself. It has been well said on this point, that God has already given Christ to the world (Jno. 3:16), but that each individual must appropriate Him by a personal act to get the personal advantage of the gift, and so must each individual personally appropriate God's gift of the Holy Spirit to get the personal advantage of it. But it is argued still further that each believer has the Holy Spirit. This is also true in a sense. "If any man have not the Spirit of Christ, he is none of His. (Rom. 8:9.) But as we have already seen, it is quite possible to have something, yes much, of the Spirit's presence and work in the heart, and yet come short of that special fulness and work known in the Bible as the Baptism or Filling with the Holy Spirit. In answer to all specious reasonings on this subject we put the simple statement of Christ: "How much more shall your heavenly Father give the Holy Spirit to them that *ask* Him." At a convention at which the author was announced to speak on this subject, a brother said to him: "I see you are to speak on the Baptism with the Holy Spirit." "Yes." "It is the most important subject on the programme; now be sure and tell them not to pray for the Holy Spirit." "I shall certainly not tell them that; for Jesus said: ' How much more shall your heavenly Father give the Holy Spirit to them that *ask* Him.'" "Oh, but that was before Pentecost." "How about Acts 4: 31? Was that before Pentecost or after?" "After it, of course." "Well, read it." It was read: "When they had *prayed*, the place was shaken where they were assembled together, and they were all filled with the Holy Ghost." "How about the eighth chapter of Acts? Was that before Pentecost or after?" "After, of course?" "Well, read the fourteenth to the seventeenth verses." The verses were read: "Peter and John, when they were come down, *prayed* for them, that they *might receive the Holy Ghost; for as yet He was fallen upon none of them*, . . . and they received the Holy Ghost." Against all inferences is this clear teaching of the Word by precept and example, that the Holy Spirit is given in answer to prayer. It was so at Pentecost; it has been so since. Those whom I have met who give most evidence of the Spirit's presence and power in their life and work believe in praying for the Holy Spirit. It has been the author's unspeakable privilege to pray with many ministers and Christian workers for this great blessing, and afterward to learn from them or from others of the new power that has come into their service, none other than the power of the Holy Spirit.

7. The seventh and last step is found in Mark 11:24. "What things soever ye desire, when ye pray, *believe* that ye receive them, and ye shall have them." God's most positive and unqualified promises must be appropriated by faith. In Jas. 1:5, we read: "If any of you lack wisdom, let him ask of God that giveth to all men liberally and upbraideth not; and it shall be given him." Now, that is certainly positive and unqualified enough, but listen to what the writer says next: "But let him ask *in faith, nothing wavering,* for he that wavereth is like a wave of the sea driven with the wind and tossed. For let not that man think that he shall receive anything of the Lord." There must then be faith in order to make our own the most positive and unqualified promises of God, such as that in Luke 11:13, and Acts 2:38, 39. Here then we discover the cause of failure, in many cases, to enter into the blessing of the Baptism with the Holy Spirit. The failure is because the last step is not taken—the simple step of faith. They do not believe, they do not confidently expect, and we have another instance of how men "Entered not in because of unbelief."

(Heb. 4: 6.) There are many, very many, who are kept out of this land of milk and honey just by this unbelief. It should be added that there is a faith that goes beyond expectation, a faith that just puts out its hand and takes what it asks. This is brought out very clearly by the R. V. of Mark 11: 24. "All things whatsoever ye pray and ask for, believe that ye have received them and ye shall have them." I remember how greatly I was perplexed by this rendering of the R. V. when I first noticed it. On examining the Greek of the passage I saw that the R. V. was correct, but what did it mean? It seemed like a singular confusion of the tenses. "Believe that ye *have* (already) *received* them, and ye *shall have* them." This seeming enigma was solved long after, while studying the First Epistle of John. I read in the fifth chapter, fourteenth and fifteenth verses: "This is the boldness which we have toward Him, that, if we ask anything according to His will, He heareth us: and if we know that He heareth us whatsoever we ask, we know that *we have* the petitions which we have asked of Him." (R. V.) When I ask anything of God the first thing to find out is: is this petition according to His will? When that is settled, when I find it is according to His will, when, for example, the thing asked is definitely promised in His Word —then I know the prayer is heard, and I know further, "I have the petition which I have asked of Him." "I know it because He plainly says so, and what I have thus appropriated on simple, childlike faith in His naked Word "I shall have" in actual experience. When one who has a clear title to a piece of property deeds it to me, it is mine as soon as the deed is properly executed and recorded, though it may be some time before I enter into the experimental enjoyment of it. I have it in the one sense as soon as the deed is recorded. I shall have it in the other sense later. In like manner, as soon as we, having met the conditions of prevailing prayer, put up to God a petition for "anything according to His will," it is our privilege to know that the prayer is heard, and that the thing which we have asked of Him is ours. Now apply this to the Baptism with the Holy Spirit. I have met the conditions of obtaining this blessing already mentioned. I simply, definitely, ask God, the Father, for the Baptism with the Holy Spirit. Then I stop and say: was that prayer "according to His will?" Yes, Luke 11: 13 says so. "If ye then being evil, know how to give good gifts unto your children, how much more shall your heavenly Father give the Holy Spirit to them that ask Him?" Acts 2: 38, 39 says: "Repent ye, and be baptised every one of you in the name of Jesus Christ unto the remission of your sins; and ye shall receive the gift of the Holy Ghost. For to you is the promise, and to your children, and to all that are afar off, even as many as the Lord our God shall call unto Him." (R. V.) It is clear that the prayer for the Baptism with the Holy Spirit is "according to His will," for it is definitely and plainly promised. I know then that the prayer is heard, and that *I have the petition which I have asked of him.* (1 Jno. 5: 14, 15, R. V.) That is, I have the Baptism with the Holy Spirit. I have then the right to arise from my knees and say, on the all=sufficient authority of God's Word: "I have the Baptism with the Holy Spirit," and *afterwards* I shall have in experimental enjoyment what I have appropriated by simple faith; for God has said, and He cannot lie, "All things whatsoever ye pray and ask for, believe that ye have received them, *and ye shall have them.*"

Any reader of this book may at this point lay it down, and, if Christ has been accepted as Savior and Lord, and openly confessed as such in God's way, and if sin has been searched out and put away, and if there has been total surrender of the will and of self to

God, and if there is a true desire, for God's glory, to be baptised with the Holy Spirit—if these conditions have been met, you may get down just now before God, and ask him to baptize you with the Holy Spirit, and you can then say, when the prayer has gone up: "That prayer was heard, I have what I have asked, I *have the baptism with the Holy Spirit*," and you have a right to get up and go out to your work, assured that in that work you will have the Holy Spirit's power. But some one will ask: "Must I not know that I have the Baptism with the Holy Spirit before I begin the work?" Certainly, but how shall we know? I know of no better way of knowing anything than by God's Word. I would believe God's Word before my feelings any day. How do we deal with an inquirer who has accepted Christ, but who lacks assurance that he has eternal life? We do not ask him to look at his feelings, but we take him to some such passage as Jno. 3: 36. We tell him to read it and he reads: "He that believeth on the Son hath everlasting life." "Who says that?" we ask. "God says it." "Is it true?" "Oh, certainly it is true; God says it." "Who does God say has everlasting life?" "He that believeth on the Son." "Do you believe on the Son?" "Yes," "What have you then?" "O, I don't know, I don't feel yet that I have eternal life." "But what does God say?" "He that believeth on the Son hath everlasting life." "Are you going to believe God or your feelings?" We hold the inquirer right there until on the simple, naked Word of God, feeling or no feeling, he says: "I know I have eternal life because God says so," and afterwards the feeling comes. Deal with yourself in this matter of the Baptism with the Holy Spirit just as you deal with an inquirer in the matter of assurance. *Be sure you have met the conditions,* and then simply *ask, claim, act.* But some one will say: "Will it be just as it was before; will there not be some manifestation?" Most assuredly there will be some manifestation. "To each one is given the manifestation of the Spirit to profit withal." (1 Cor. 12:7, R. V.) But what will the character of the manifestation be and where shall we see it? It is at this point that many make a mistake. They have, perhaps, read the life of Mr. Finney or of Jonathan Edwards, and recall how great waves of electric emotion swept over these men until they were obliged to ask God to withdraw His hand lest they die from the ecstacy. Or they have gone to some meeting, and heard testimonies to similar experiences, and they expect something like this. Now I do not deny the reality of such experiences. I cannot. The testimony of such men as Finney and Edwards is to be believed. There is a stronger reason why I cannot deny them. But while admitting the reality of these experiences, I would ask, where is there a single line of the New Testament that describes any such experience in connection with the Baptism with the Holy Spirit? Every manifestation of the Baptism with the Holy Spirit in the New Testament was in new power in service. Look, for example, at 1 Cor. 12, where this subject is treated in the most thorough way, look also at Acts 2:4; 4:31; 4:33; 9:17, 22 and note the the character of the manifestations mentioned. It is quite probable that the Apostles had similar experiences to those of Finney and Edwards and others, but, if they had, the Holy Spirit kept them from recording them. It is well He did; for, if they had told of such things, we would have looked for these things rather than the more important manifestation of power in service.

But another question will be asked: "Did not the Apostles wait ten days, and may we not have to wait?" The Apostles were kept waiting ten days, but the reason is given in Acts 2:1: "When the Day of Pentecost was now come" (literally was being fulfilled, R. V. Marg.) In

HOW BAPTISM MAY BE OBTAINED 59

the eternal purposes and plans of God, and in the Old Testament types, the Day of Pentecost was set as the time for the giving of the Holy Spirit, and the Spirit could not be given until the Day of Pentecost was fully come, but we read of no waiting after Pentecost. In Acts 4:31 there was no waiting. "*When they had prayed* the place was shaken where they were assembled together, and they were all filled with the Holy Ghost." In Acts 8 there was no waiting. When Peter and John came down to Samaria, and found that none of the young converts had been baptized with the Holy Spirit, they "prayed for them, that they might receive the Holy Ghost," and they did then and there. (Acts 8: 15, 17). Paul of Tarsus was not obliged to wait, in the ninth chapter of the Acts. Ananias came in and told him of this wondrous gift, and baptized him, and laid his hands upon him, and "*straightway* in the synagogue he proclaimed Jesus, that He is the Son of God." (Acts 9:17, 20). There was no waiting in Acts 10. Before Peter had fairly gotten through his sermon the Baptism with the Holy Spirit came. (Acts 10:44–46; Comp. Chap. 11:15, 16.) In the nineteenth chapter of the Acts there was no waiting. As soon as Paul had declared to the Ephesian disciples the gift of the Holy Spirit, and the conditions were met, the blessing followed. (Acts 19:1-6.) Men have to wait only when they do not meet the conditions, when Christ is not fully accepted, or sin is not put away, or there is not total surrender, or true desire, or definite prayer, or simple faith, just taking upon the naked Word. The absence of some of these things keeps many waiting for more than ten days sometimes. But there is no need that any reader of this book wait ten hours. You can have the Baptism with the Holy Spirit just now, if you will. A young man once came to me in great earnestness about this matter. "I heard of the Baptism with the Holy Spirit," he said, "some time ago, and have been seeking it, but have not received it." "Is your will laid down?" "I am afraid that is the trouble." "Will you lay it down?" "I am afraid I cannot." "Are you willing God should lay it down for you?" "Yes." "Ask Him to." We knelt in prayer, and he asked God to lay down his will for him. "Did God hear that prayer?" "He must have, it was according to His will." "Is your will laid down?" "It must be." "Then ask God for the Baptism with the Holy Spirit." He did this. "Was that prayer according to His will?" "Yes." "Was it heard?" "It must have been." "Have you the Baptism with the Holy Spirit?" "I don't feel it." "That is not what I asked you; read those verses again." The Bible lay open before him at 1 Jno. 5: 14, 15, and he read: "This is the confidence we have in Him that, if we ask anything according to His will, He heareth us." "Wait a moment; was that prayer according to His will?" "It certainly was." "Was it heard?" "It was." "Read on." "And if we know that He hears us whatsoever we ask, we know that we have the petitions that we desired of Him." "Know what?" "That we have the petitions we desired of Him." "What was the petition?" "The Baptism with the Holy Spirit." Have you it?" "I don't feel it, but God says so, and I must have." A few days later I met him again, and asked if he really had received what he took on simple faith. With a happy look in his face he answered, "Yes." I lost sight of him for perhaps two years, and then found him preparing for the ministry and already preaching, and God was honoring his preaching with souls saved, and a little later used him with others as a means of great blessing to the theological seminary where he was studying. He had also decided to serve Christ in the foreign field. What he claimed on simple faith and received, any reader of this book can claim and receive in the same way.

I would not say a word to dissuade men from spending much time in waiting upon God in prayer. "They that wait upon the Lord shall renew their strength." (Is. 40: 31.) There are few of us indeed in these days who spend as many hours as we should in waiting upon God. The writer can bear joyful testimony to the manifest outpourings of the Spirit that have come, time and again, as he has waited upon God though the hours of the night with believing brethren. But there are, I am persuaded, many waiting for feeling that ought to be claiming by faith.

CHAPTER IV

"FRESH BAPTISMS WITH THE HOLY SPIRIT," OR THE REFILLING WITH THE HOLY SPIRIT

In the second chapter of the Acts of the Apostles, fourth verse, we read: "They were all filled with the Holy Ghost, and began to speak,' etc. This was the fulfilment of Acts 1: 5. "Ye shall be baptized with the Holy Ghost not many days hence." One of those mentioned by name as being "filled with the Holy Ghost,' (Acts 2:4,) or " baptised with the Holy Ghost' (Acts 1:5), at this time was Peter. Turning over to the fourth chapter, the eight verse, we read: " Then Peter, filled with the Holy Ghost, said unto them," etc. Here Peter experienced a new filling with the Holy Spirit. Again, in the thirty-first verse of the same chapter, we read: " When they had prayed, the place was shaken where they were assembled together; and they were all filled with the Holy Ghost." Peter is named as one of this company (verses 19 and 23), so we see that Peter here experienced a third filling with the Holy Spirit. It is evident that it is not sufficient that one be once "baptized with the Holy Spirit." As new emergencies of service arise, there must be new fillings with the Spirit. The failure to realize this has led to most sad and serious results in many a man's service. He has been baptized at some period in his life with the Holy Spirit, and strives to get though his whole future life in the power of this past experience. It is largely for this reason, that we see so many men who once unquestionably worked in the Holy Spirit's power, who give little evidence of the possession of that power to-day. For each new service that is to be conducted, for each new soul that is to be dealt with, for each new service for Christ that is to be performed, for each new day and each new emergency of Christian life and service, we should definitely seek a new filling with the Holy Spirit. I do not deny that there is an "anointing that abideth," (1 Jno. 2: 27), nor the permanency of the gifts that the Holy Spirit bestows; I simply assert with clear and abundant Scripture proof, to say nothing of proof from experience and observation, that this gift must not be "neglected," (1 Tim. 4: 14) but rather "kindled anew" or "stirred into flame" (2 Tim. 1: 6, R. V. Marg.); and that repeated fillings with the Holy Spirit are necessary to continuance and increase of power. Now arises the question, ought these new *fillings* with the Holy Spirit to be called "fresh *Baptisms* with the Holy Spirit?" While, on the one hand, it must be admitted that in Acts 2: 4, the expression, "*filled* with the Holy Ghost," is used to describe the experience promised in Acts 1:5, in the words: "Ye shall be *baptized* with the Holy Ghost," and that therefore the two expressions are to this extent synonymous; on the other hand, it should be noticed, that the expression, "Baptized with the Holy Spirit," is nowhere used in the Bible of any experience but the first, and that, furthermore, the word "baptized" of itself suggests an initial or initiatory experience. While, therefore, we stand for the truth that those who speak of "fresh baptisms with the Holy Spirit" are aiming at, it would seem wisest to follow the uniform Bible usage, and speak of the experiences that succeed the first, as being "*filled* with the Holy Spirit," and not as being "baptized with the Holy Spirit."

CHAPTER V

HOW SPIRITUAL POWER IS LOST

Any discussion of the Baptism with the Holy Spirit, and the power which results from it, would be incomplete, if attention were not called to the fact that spiritual power may be lost.

One of the strangest and saddest stories of the Old Testament history, is that of Samson. It is also one of the most instructive. He was by far the most remarkable man of his day. The grandest opportunities were open to him, but after striking temporary victories, his life ended in tragic failure, all through his own inexcusable folly. Time and again it is said of him that "the Spirit of the Lord came mightily upon him," and in the power of that Spirit he wrought to the astonishment of his people and the discomfiture of the enemies of the Lord; but in Judges 16:19, 20, we see him deserted of the Lord, though unconscious of it, his strength gone from him, and he about to be taken into wretched captivity, the sport of the godless, and

HOW SPIRITUAL POWER IS LOST 67

to die with the enemies of the Lord a violent and dishonored death.

Unfortunately Samson is not the only man in Christian history, who, having once known the power of the Holy Spirit, has afterward been shorn of this power and laid aside. There have been many Samsons, and I presume there will be many more—men whom God has once used mightily and has afterward been forced to lay aside. One of the saddest sights on earth is such a man. Let us consider when it is that the Lord departs from a man or withdraws His power from him, or in other words, " How power is lost."

1. *First of all God withdraws His power from men when they go back upon their separation to Him.* This was the precise case with Samson himself. (Judges 16:19, Comp. Num. 6:2, 5.) His uncut hair was the outward sign of his Nazarite vow by which "he separated himself unto the Lord." The shearing of his hair was the surrender of his separation. His separation given up he was shorn of his power. It is at this same point that many a man to-day is shorn of his power. There was a day when he separated himself unto God. He turned his back utterly upon the world and its ambitions, its spirit, its purposes; he set himself apart to God as holy unto Him, to be His, for God to take

him and use him and do with him what He would. God has honored his separation, He has anointed him with the Holy Ghost and power. He has been used of God. But Delilah has come to him. The world has captured his heart again. He has listened to the world's siren voice, and allowed her to shear him of the sign of separation. He is no longer a man separated, or wholly consecrated, to the Lord, and the Lord leaves him. Are there not such persons among those who read this? Men and women the Lord once used, but He does not use you now. You may still be outwardly in Christian work, but there is not the old time liberty and power in it, and this is the reason—you have been untrue to your separation, to your consecration to God; you are listening to Delilah, to the voice of the harlot, to the world and its allurements. Would you get the old power back again? There is but one thing to do. Let your hair grow again as Samson did. Renew your consecration to God.

2. *Power is lost through the incoming of sin.* It was so with Saul, the son of Kish. The Spirit of God came upon Saul and he wrought a great victory for God. (1 Samuel 11:6, ff.) He brought the people of God forward to a place of triumph over their enemies, who had held

HOW SPIRITUAL POWER IS LOST 69

them under for years. But Saul disobeyed God in two distinct instances (1 Samuel 13:13, 14; 15:3, 9-11, 23), and the Lord withdrew His favor and His power, and Saul's life ended in utter defeat and ruin. This is the history of many men whom God has once used. Sin has crept in. They have done that which God has told them not to do, or they have refused to do that which God bade them do, and the power of God has been withdrawn. The one who has known God's power in service, and would continue to know it, must walk very softly before Him. He must be listening constantly to hear what God bids him do or not do. He must respond promptly to the slightest whisper of God. It would seem as if any one who had once known God's power would rather die than lose it. But it is lost through the incoming of sin. Are there those among the readers of this book who are passing through this dreadful experience of the loss of God's power? Ask yourself if this be the reason; has sin crept in somewhere? Are you doing something, some little thing, perhaps, that God tells you not to do? Are you leaving undone something God bids you do? Set this matter right with God and the old power will come back. David was guilty of an awful sin, but when that sin was confessed and put away, he came to know again the power of the Spirit. (Ps. 32:1–5; 51:11–13.)

If we would continuously know the power of God we should go often alone with Him, at the close of each day at least, and ask Him to show us if any sin, anything displeasing in His sight, has crept in that day, and if He shows us that there has, we should confess it and put it away then and there.

3. *Power is lost again through self=indul= gence.* The one who would have God's power must lead a life of self=denial. There are many things which are not sinful in the ordinary understanding of the word sin, but which hinder spirituality and rob men of power. I do not believe that any man can lead a luxurious life, over=indulge his natural appetites, indulge extensively in dainties, and enjoy the fulness of God's power. The gratification of the flesh and the fulness of the Spirit, do not go hand in hand. "The flesh lusteth against the Spirit, and the Spirit against the flesh: and these two are contrary the one to the other." (Gal 5:17.) Paul wrote, "I keep under my body, and bring it into subjection." (1 Cor. 9:27, see R. V, Greek. Note also Eph. 5:18.)

We live in a day when the temptation to the

indulgence of the flesh is very great. Luxuries are common. Piety and prosperity not seldom go hand in hand, and, in many a case, the prosperity that piety and power have brought has been the ruin of the man to whom it has come. Not a few ministers of power have become popular and in demand. With the increasing popularity has come an increase of pay and of the comforts of life. Luxurious living has come in, and the power of the Spirit has gone out. It would not be difficult to cite specific instances of this sad truth. If we would know the continuance of the Spirit's power, we need to be on guard to lead lives of simplicity, free from indulgence and surfeiting, ever ready to "endure hardness, as a good soldier of Jesus Christ." (2 Tim. 2: 3.) I frankly confess I am afraid of luxury;— not as afraid of it as I am of sin. but it comes next as an object of dread. It is very subtle but a very potent enemy of power. There are devils to-day that "go not out but by prayer and fasting."

4. *Power is lost through greed for money.* It was through this that a member of the original Apostolic company, the twelve whom Jesus Himself chose to be with Him, fell. The love of money, the love of accumulation, got into the heart of Judas Iscariot, and proved his ruin.

"The love of money is a root of all kinds of evil," (1 Tim. 6: 10, R. V.) but one of the greatest evils of which it is the root is that of the loss of spiritual power. How many a man there is to-day who once knew what spiritual power was, but money began to come. He soon felt its strange fascination. The love for accumulation, covetousness, the love for more, little by little took possession of him. He has accumulated his money honestly; but it has absorbed him, and the Spirit of God is shut out and His power has departed. Men who would have power, need to have the words of Christ. "Take heed and beware of covetousness," writ large and graved deep upon their hearts. One does not need to be rich to be covetous. A very poor man may be very much absorbed in the desire for wealth—just as much so as any greedy millionaire.

5. *Power is lost through pride.* This is the subtlest and most dangerous of all the enemies of power. I am not sure but that more men lose their power at this point, than at any of those mentioned thus far. There is many a man who has not consciously gone back upon his consecration, he has not let sin, in the sense of conscious doing of that which God forbade or conscious refusal to do that which God com-

HOW SPIRITUAL POWER IS LOST 73

manded, creep into his life, he has not given way to self-indulgence; he has utterly, persistently and consistently refused the allurements of money accumulation, but still he has failed; *pride has come in.* He has become puffed up because of the very fact that God has given him power and used him; puffed up, it may be, over the consistency and simplicity and devotion of his life; and God has been forced to set him aside. God cannot use a proud man. (1 Pet. 5: 5.) "God resisteth the proud and giveth grace to the humble." The man who is puffed up with pride, self-esteem, cannot be filled up with the Holy Spirit. Paul saw this danger for himself. God saw it for him, and "lest he be exalted above measure, through the abundance of the revelations, there was given to (him) a thorn in the flesh, the messenger of Satan to buffet (him), lest (he) should be exalted above measure." (2 Cor. 12: 7.) How many men have failed here! They have sought God's power, sought it in God's way, it has come. Men have testified of the blessing received through their word, and pride has entered and been indulged, and all is lost. Moses was the meekest of men, and yet he failed at this very point. "Must we fetch you water out of this rock?" he cried, and then and there God laid him aside. (Num. 20:10-12.) If God is using us at all, let us get down very low before Him. The more he uses us the lower let us get. May God keep His own Words ringing in our ears: "Be clothed with humility, for God resisteth the proud, and giveth grace to the humble." (1 Pet. 5:5.)

6. *Power is lost through neglect of prayer.* It is in prayer especially that we are charged with the energy of God. It is the man who is much in prayer into whom God's power flows mightily. John Livingston spent a night with some Christians in conference and prayer. The next day June 21st, 1630, he so preached at the Kirk of Shotts, that the Spirit fell upon his hearers in such a way that five hundred could either date their conversion or some remarkable confirmation from that day forward. This is but one instance among thousands to show how power is given in prayer. Virtue or power is constantly going from us, as from Christ (Mark 5:30), in service and blessing; and if power would be maintained, it must be constantly renewed in prayer. When electricity is given off from a charged body it must be recharged. So must we be recharged with the Divine energy, and this is effected by coming into contact with God in prayer. Many a man whom God has

used has become lax in his habits of prayer, and the Lord departs from him and his power is gone. Are there not some of us who have not to-day the power we once had, and simply because we do not spend the time on our faces before God that we once did?

7. *Power is lost through neglect of the Word.* God's power comes through prayer, it comes also through the Word (Ps. 1:2, 3; Josh. 1:8.) Many have known the power that comes through the regular, thoughtful, prayerful, protracted meditation upon the Word, but business and perhaps Christian duties have multiplied, other studies have come in, the Word has been in a measure crowded out, and power has gone. We must meditate daily, prayerfully, profoundly upon the Word if we are to maintain power. Many a man has run dry through its neglect.

I think the seven points mentioned give the principal ways in which spiritual power is lost. I think of no others. If there is one dread that comes to me more frequently than any other, it is that of losing the power of God. Oh, the agony of having known God's power, of having been used of Him, and then of having that power withdrawn, to be laid aside as far as any real usefulness is concerned. Men may still praise you, but God can't use you. To see a perishing world around you and to know there is no power in your words to save. Would not to die be better than that? I have little fear of losing eternal life. Every believer in Christ has that already. I am in the hand of Jesus Christ, and in the hand of God the Father, and no one can pluck me out of Their hand, (John 10: 28, 29), *but* I see so many men from whom God has departed, men once eminently used of God, I walk with fear and trembling, and cry unto Him daily to keep me from the things that would make the withdrawal of His power necessary. But what those things are I think He has made plain to me, and I have tried in the words here written to make them plain to both you and myself. To sum them up they are these: the surrender of our separation, sin, self-indulgence, greed for money, pride, the neglect of prayer, and the neglect of the Word. Shall we not, by God's grace, from this time be on our guard against these things, and thus make sure of the continuance of God's power in our life and service until that glad day comes when we can say with Paul: "I have fought a good fight, I have finished my course, I have kept the faith; henceforth there is laid up for me a crown of righteousness, which the Lord, the righteous judge, shall give me at that day,"

(2 Tim. 4:7, 8), or better yet with Jesus, "I have glorified Thee on the earth, having accomplished the work which Thou hast given me to do." (Jno. 17:4, R. V.)

FINIS.

TITLES in THIS SERIES

1. THE HIGHER CHRISTIAN LIFE; A BIBLIOGRAPHICAL OVERVIEW. Donald W. Dayton, *THE AMERICAN HOLINESS MOVEMENT: A BIBLIOGRAPHICAL INTRODUCTION.* (Wilmore, Ky., 1971) *bound with* David W. Faupel, *THE AMERICAN PENTECOSTAL MOVEMENT: A BIBLIOGRAPHICAL ESSAY.* (Wilmore, Ky., 1972) *bound with* David D. Bundy, *Keswick: A BIBLIOGRAPHIC INTRODUCTION TO THE HIGHER LIFE MOVEMENTS.* (Wilmore, Ky., 1975)

2. *ACCOUNT OF THE UNION MEETING FOR THE PROMOTION OF SCRIPTURAL HOLINESS, HELD AT OXFORD, AUGUST 29 TO SEPTEMBER 7, 1874.* (Boston, n. d.)

3. Baker, Elizabeth V., and Co-workers, *CHRONICLES OF A FAITH LIFE.*

4. THE WORK OF T. B. BARRATT. T. B. Barratt, *IN THE DAYS OF THE LATTER RAIN.* (London, 1909) *WHEN THE FIRE FELL AND AN OUTLINE OF MY LIFE*, (Oslo, 1927)

5. WITNESS TO PENTECOST: THE LIFE OF FRANK BARTLEMAN. Frank Bartleman, *FROM PLOW TO PULPIT—FROM MAINE TO CALIFORNIA* (Los Angeles, n. d.), *HOW PENTECOST CAME TO LOS ANGELES* (Los An-

geles, 1925), *Around the World by Faith, With Six Weeks in the Holy Land* (Los Angeles, n. d.), *Two Years Mission Work in Europe Just before the World War, 1912-14* (Los Angeles, [1926])

6. Boardman, W. E., *The Higher Christian Life* (Boston, 1858)

7. Girvin, E. A., *Phineas F. Bresee: A Prince In Israel* (Kansas City, Mo., [1916])

8. Brooks, John P., *The Divine Church* (Columbia, Mo., 1891)

9. Russell Kelso Carter on "Faith Healing." R. Kelso Carter, *The Atonement for Sin and Sickness* (Boston, 1884) *"Faith Healing" Reviewed After Twenty Years* (Boston, 1897)

10. Daniels, W. H., *Dr. Cullis and His Work* (Boston, [1885])

11. Holiness Tracts Defending the Ministry of Women. Luther Lee, *"Woman's Right to Preach the Gospel; a Sermon, at the Ordination of Rev. Miss Antoinette L. Brown, at South Butler, Wayne County, N. Y., Sept. 15, 1853"* (Syracuse, 1853) *bound with* B. T. Roberts, *Ordaining Women* (Rochester, 1891) *bound with* Catherine (Mumford) Booth, *"Female Ministry; or, Woman's Right to Preach the Gospel . . ."* (London, n. d.) *bound with* Fannie (McDowell) Hunter, *Women Preachers* (Dallas, 1905)

12. Late Nineteenth Century Revivalist Teachings on the Holy Spirit. D. L. Moody, *Secret Power or the Secret of Success in Christian Life and*

Work (New York, [1881]) *bound with* J. Wilbur Chapman, *Received Ye the Holy Ghost?* (New York, [1894]) *bound with* R. A. Torrey, *The Baptism with the Holy Spirit* (New York, 1895 & 1897)

13. Seven "Jesus Only" Tracts. Andrew D. Urshan, *The Doctrine of the New Birth, or, the Perfect Way to Eternal Life* (Cochrane, Wis., 1921) *bound with* Andrew Urshan, *The Almighty God in the Lord Jesus Christ* (Los Angeles, 1919) *bound with* Frank J. Ewart, *The Revelation of Jesus Christ* (St. Louis, n. d.) *bound with* G. T. Haywood, *The Birth of the Spirit in the Days of the Apostles* (Indianapolis, n. d.) *Divine Names and Titles of Jehovah* (Indianapolis, n. d.) *The Finest of the Wheat* (Indianapolis, n. d.) *The Victim of the Flaming Sword* (Indianapolis, n. d.)

14. Three Early Pentecostal Tracts. D. Wesley Myland, *The Latter Rain Covenant and Pentecostal Power* (Chicago, 1910) *bound with* G. F. Taylor, *The Spirit and the Bride* (n. p., [1907?]) *bound with* B. F. Laurence, *The Apostolic Faith Restored* (St. Louis, 1916)

15. Fairchild, James H., *Oberlin: The Colony and the College, 1833-1883* (Oberlin, 1883)

16. Figgis, John B., *Keswick from Within* (London, [1914])

17. Finney, Charles G., *Lectures to Professing Christians* (New York, 1837)

18. Fleisch, Paul, *Die Moderne Gemeinschaftsbewegung in Deutschland* (Leipzig, 1912)

19. SIX TRACTS BY W. B. GODBEY. *SPIRITUAL GIFTS AND GRACES* (Cincinnati, [1895]) *THE RETURN OF JESUS* (Cincinnati, [1899?]) *WORK OF THE HOLY SPIRIT* (Louisville, [1902]) *CHURCH—BRIDE—KINGDOM* (Cincinnati, [1905]) *DIVINE HEALING* (Greensboro, [1909]) *TONGUE MOVEMENT, SATANIC* (Zarephath, N. J., 1918)

20. Gordon, Earnest B., *ADONIRAM JUDSON GORDON* (New York, [1896])

21. Hills, A. M., *HOLINESS AND POWER FOR THE CHURCH AND THE MINISTRY* (Cincinnati, [1897])

22. Horner, Ralph C., *FROM THE ALTAR TO THE UPPER ROOM* (Toronto, [1891])

23. McDonald, William and John E. Searles, *THE LIFE OF REV. JOHN S. INSKIP* (Boston, [1885])

24. LaBerge, Agnes N. O., *WHAT GOD HATH WROUGHT* (Chicago, n. d.)

25. Lee, Luther, *AUTOBIOGRAPHY OF THE REV. LUTHER LEE* (New York, 1882)

26. McLean, A. and J. W. Easton, *PENUEL; OR, FACE TO FACE WITH GOD* (New York, 1869)

27. McPherson, Aimee Semple, *THIS IS THAT: PERSONAL EXPERIENCES SERMONS AND WRITINGS* (Los Angeles, [1919])

28. Mahan, Asa, *OUT OF DARKNESS INTO LIGHT* (London, 1877)

29. THE LIFE AND TEACHING OF CARRIE JUDD MONTGOMERY Carrie Judd Montgomery, *"UNDER HIS WINGS": THE STORY OF MY LIFE* (Oakland,

[1936]) Carrie F. Judd, *The Prayer of Faith* (New York, 1880)

30. THE DEVOTIONAL WRITINGS OF PHOEBE PALMER Phoebe Palmer, *The Way of Holiness* (52nd ed., New York, 1867) *Faith and Its Effects* (27th ed., New York, n. d., orig. pub. 1854)

31. Wheatley, Richard, *The Life and Letters of Mrs. Phoebe Palmer* (New York, 1881)

32. Palmer, Phoebe, ed., *Pioneer Experiences* (New York, 1868)

33. Palmer, Phoebe, *The Promise of the Father* (Boston, 1859)

34. Pardington, G. P., *Twenty-five Wonderful Years, 1889-1914: A Popular Sketch of the Christian and Missionary Alliance* (New York, [1914])

35. Parham, Sarah E., *The Life of Charles F. Parham, Founder of the Apostolic Faith Movement* (Joplin, [1930])

36. THE SERMONS OF CHARLES F. PARHAM. Charles F. Parham, *A Voice Crying in the Wilderness* (4th ed., Baxter Springs, Kan., 1944, orig. pub. 1902) *The Everlasting Gospel* (n.p., n.d., orig. pub. 1911)

37. Pierson, Arthur Tappan, *Forward Movements of the Last Half Century* (New York, 1905)

38. *Proceedings of Holiness Conferences, Held at Cincinnati, November 26th, 1877, and at New York, December 17th, 1877* (Philadelphia, 1878)

39. *Record of the Convention for the Promotion of*

Scriptural Holiness Held at Brighton, May 29th, to June 7th, 1875 (Brighton, [1896?])

40. Rees, Seth Cook, *Miracles in the Slums* (Chicago, [1905?])

41. Roberts, B. T., *Why Another Sect* (Rochester, 1879)

42. Shaw, S. B., ed., *Echoes of the General Holiness Assembly* (Chicago, [1901])

43. *The Devotional Writings of Robert Pearsall Smith and Hannah Whitall Smith.* [R]obert [P]earsall [S]mith, *Holiness Through Faith: Light on the Way of Holiness* (New York, [1870]) [H]annah [W]hitall [S]mith, *The Christian's Secret of a Happy Life,* (Boston and Chicago, [1885])

44. [S]mith, [H]annah [W]hitall, *The Unselfishness of god and How I Discovered It* (New York, [1903])

45. Steele, Daniel, *A Substitute for Holiness; or, Antinomianism Revived* (Chicago and Boston, [1899])

46. Tomlinson, A. J., *The Last Great Conflict* (Cleveland, 1913)

47. Upham, Thomas C., *The Life of Faith* (Boston, 1845)

48. Washburn, Josephine M., *History and Reminiscences of the Holiness Church Work in Southern California and Arizona* (South Pasadena, [1912?])

LIBRARY OF DAVIDSON COLLEGE